11/14/84

For David,

Bon Appetit!

Jane Hibler

Easy and Elegant
SEAFOOD

AN EVERYDAY GUIDE TO BUYING AND COOKING SEAFOOD AND FISH

Jane Franke Hibler

Color Photos by Mike Henley

Frank Amato Publications
P. O. Box 02112, Portland, Oregon 97202
(503) 653-8108

Dedication

This book
is dedicated to the two processors,
specifically the food processor and the word processor,
which have made cooking and writing an even more joyful
part of my life.

Copyright 1984 Jane Franke Hibler   Printed in the United States of America

ISBN 0-936608-30-7   Book Design: Kathy Johnson   Typesetting: Chris Mazzuca

Table of Contents

Acknowledgments 6
Author's Note 7
A Step To Good Health 8
Introduction 9
Secrets to Successful Fish Cookery . 11
Some Fishy Information 21
Appetizers 42
Salads 57
Soups 84
Entrées 92
Stocks 127
Sauces 129
Smoking Fish 135
Bibliography 139
Index 140

Acknowledgments

I am grateful to the following people for their assistance with this book: Gary Hibler for his many hours of editing and sacrificing his free time to go fishing; Frank Amato for having such a hearty appetite that this book sounded like a good idea; Renée Glasgow and Terry Farrens for their valuable editing assistance; Michelle Tennyson for her wealth of information on fish resources; the Ferrens and the Waltas for the loan of their dishes for the photographs; the Moore Company of Portland for providing a Sharp microwave for recipe testing; and to photographer Mike Henley for his deliciously clear pictures.

Author's Note

Does confusion ever strike when you walk into a fish market and see any of the following: five types of sole; three species of fresh salmon, kippered salmon and lox; two sizes of scallops; fourteen jars of oysters, bay shrimp that you have always called cocktail shrimp; and lingcod and "true cod" which don't look anything alike? If so, then this book is for you. It will ease your unnecessary anxieties and provide you with information about seafood and fish you have always wanted to know but were too intimidated to ask. Included in the book is a brief sketch about many of our most popular culinary fish and instructions on how to buy and cook them.

It will also supply you with many new and exciting fish recipes to keep abused tastebuds from going on strike. These recipes have been developed during the past six years while teaching seafood classes and have been tested over and over again by many unsuspecting students. You will find the recipes quick and easy to prepare using only the freshest ingredients and many can be assembled ahead of time. There are also microwave instructions listed when possible.

I hope this book inspires you to take full advantage of the bountiful supply of fresh fish and seafood available today. Let it be your guide to creative and successful fish cookery.

A Step To Good Health

There are many reasons to eat fish and shellfish. First and foremost is that they taste good. They are also easy to prepare and do not require a lengthy cooking process. And, there are definite side benefits from eating these creatures that inhabit the Earth's waters. They are an excellent source of protein, rich in phosphorus, iodine, calcium, iron and copper and they contain fish oil. Dietary fish oil has also been proven to actually lower the plasma lipid (cholesterol and triglyceride) levels in the body thereby reducing the risk of heart disease. According to Dr. William E. Connor, M. D., Department of Medicine (Section of Clinical Nutrition and Lipid Metabolism), Oregon Health Sciences University, fish oil appears to lower plasma lipids even more effectively than vegetable oils. It also helps to prevent the formation of dangerous clots by reducing the stickiness of platelets — cells found in the bloodstream that play a major role in blood clots.

It is a relief to know that there are foods that are sinfully delicious, such as a fresh fillet of barbecued salmon, that are actually good for you. I knew if I looked long enough something would turn up!

Introduction

It is theorized that when the Earth was formed more than five billion years ago it was a swirling mass of fiery hot matter. After it solidified it took thousands of centuries for its surface to cool down; as it did, moist air condensed to form the planet's major bodies of water. Over three-fourths of the Earth's surface was covered with water, water rich with the essential ingredients of life: oxygen, hydrogen, nitrogen and carbon. With the "magic" combination of elements present, miraculously, the first one-celled organisms appeared about a billion years later.

Gradually, life forms grew more complex with the emergence of algae, plants and animals. The first fish appeared about 600 million years ago and with such a vast space and endless varieties of environments, more than 20,000 different species evolved. Out of these thousands of species only 200 or more species are eaten by man. And, out of those 200, less than half are commercially important in the American diet. The great potential of unharvested fish that could be utilized in our diets today is just now being fully realized.

The majority of fish harvested worldwide are herrings, anchovies and sardines. Over fifty million tons of fish are taken from the oceans yearly and only half of that amount is used for human consumption. Other uses of fish or fish products include the production of fish meal, fish oil, pharmaceutical drugs, pearl essence, poultry feed, liquid fish fertilizer and leather, to name a few.

Advanced technology has provided us with improved means of transporting this perishable commodity and consequently we have a greater selection of fish and shellfish in seafood markets today than we did twenty years ago.

Another boon to the industry has been the development of

aquaculture, the rearing of plants, fish and shellfish under controlled conditions. The largest aquaculture industry in the United States is located in the South and Southwest where channel catfish are raised. Other species grown through aquaculture in the United States include ninety-three types of finfish; seven types of shrimp and prawns; lobsters; mollusks; seaweed; turtles; alligators and eels. Over the last ten years domestic production has tripled, yet it is still short of supplying market needs. The fishing industry is working hard to meet the demands of the American public for their production.

Secrets to Successful Fish Cookery

How To Buy Fresh Fish

1. The eyes of the fish should be clear and full, not cloudy and sunken.
2. The flesh of the fish should not have an overpowering fishy odor; it should be firm to the touch, not soft and mushy. If you push on the flesh of a fresh fish with your finger, it should not stay indented.
3. The gills should be red. As a fish ages, the gills gradually change from red to pink to pinkish brown.
4. With the exception of shrimp and some crab, most shellfish is bought alive. Do not buy shellfish with shells that remain open once they are touched. They are probably dead.

How To Store Fresh Fish And Shellfish

If you have caught your own fish it is important that the fish be kept chilled until it is eviscerated. Bacterial spoilage caused by powerful enzymes found in the slime, gills and intestinal tract does not begin until rigor mortis has set in. By keeping the catch chilled, the deterioration is delayed. The fish should then be eviscerated as soon as possible.

It is best to buy fish fresh the day you are going to use it and keep it covered air-tight in the refrigerator at 32°F. Fish should not be kept longer than two days without being frozen.

To freeze fish, double-wrap it air-tight in freezer paper or place the fish or shellfish in freezer containers; then fill them with water. No part of the fish should contact the side of the container or the product will become freezer burned. Salmon, crab and shrimp should not be frozen for longer than one to two months. Other, less fatty fish can be frozen up to three months. All fish should be kept frozen at 4°F. or lower. If you need to thaw fish that has already been frozen, let it thaw slowly in the refrigerator to avoid unnecessary loss of moisture.

Best Cookware For Fish

Fish can be cooked in almost any type of cookware: cast iron, cast iron covered with enamel, stainless steel, copper or Teflon. It is best not to use aluminum since any acid added to the pan can discolor the food by reacting with the aluminum. I prefer cast iron covered with enamel because I use it for baking as well as on top of the stove. It is also heavy and conducts heat evenly. If you are going to sauté the fish use a sauté pan or one with low sides so you will be able to turn the fish over with ease.

Seasoning For Fish

There are many herbs that add an exciting flavor to fish or shellfish. Thanks to Scandinavian cooks, dill is one herb that has long been associated with fish cookery. It can often be purchased fresh in better produce markets and it has such a mild flavor I greatly prefer it to its powerful tasting dried counterpart, dillweed. Be sure that you do not buy the long stalks of dill used for making pickles for they have already gone to seed.

Last summer I planted lemon thyme in my garden and it is a wonderful accent to fish dishes. If you do a lot of seafood cookery it is one herb that you should make an effort to find at the nursery. I keep it in a pot in my kitchen along with tarragon, chives and rosemary. The herbs do well in the house during the colder months and when the warmer weather arrives I move them outside. All of them go well with most fish.

Parsley is one herb I always use fresh. It is inexpensive to buy and if you rinse it in cold water and keep it in an airtight jar, it will last for one month.

If I do use dried herbs I always buy them whole and crush

them myself. Many of the following recipes call for 1 teaspoon whole thyme, crushed. I measure a teaspoon of the whole herb and crush it in the palm of my hand. Herbs tend to stay fresher for longer periods of time when they are bought whole instead of ground.

How To Serve Fish

Always serve fish on warmed plates. Place your dinner plates in a 200-degree oven for five minutes before you need them. When you are ready to serve the fish dish, garnish it with a sprig of fresh parsley or a slice of lemon.

Fish can be served with a variety of accompaniments. The ubiquitous baked potato with butter and sour cream is always tasty with sautéed or grilled fish. Potatoes can also be baked and restuffed, fried, boiled, deepfried or made into potato salad. If you are going to serve fish with a sauce, good accompaniments could be a seasoned rice or one of the many varieties of pasta.

How To Cook Fish

By understanding the general composition of fish, one is more likely to have greater success with fish cookery. Almost all fish are composed of two muscles — the lateral muscle which makes up most of the fish, and a small superficial muscle found near each side of the lateral line. These muscles as well as the muscles of red meat are made up of muscle fibers. The main structural differences between red meats and fish is that fish have much shorter muscle fibers and much less connective tissue. (Connective tissue is the structural network that holds the muscle fibers together.) Also, the connective tissue of fish is broken down with heat much faster than that of red meat. What this means to the cook is that it is not necessary to marinate fish to tenderize it. The fish, because of its structural makeup, will be tender as soon as it is cooked as long as it is not *overcooked*!

The lateral muscle is usually colorless, with the exception of the salmon family, while the superficial muscle is a dark reddish brown. This dark muscle gets its color from myoglobin, a protein that supplies oxygen to the muscle, and it also contains a high proportion of fat. You have probably noticed while eating that occasionally you will eat a bite of fish that is darker than the rest of the fish and it is very fishy tasting. This is due to the high concentration of fat in the superficial muscle. Many fish cooks like to remove this muscle before cooking the fish.

    If you are cooking a thick piece of fish, test it for doneness by using a metal cake tester or a larding needle. Sometimes a fork cannot penetrate deep enough into the flesh. When the fish is done, its juices will be milky colored and it should flake easily. If you have pierced the fish and you are still in doubt as to whether the fish is done cut into the center of the fish. If the fish is cooked, it will no longer be translucent.

There are seven methods for cooking fish.

SAUTÉING
    The simplest method for cooking fish is sautéing and almost all fish and shellfish can be cooked this way. Both steaks and fillets can be sautéed successfully. Large fillets should be cut into serving size pieces. Otherwise it would be too difficult to turn the fish over halfway through the cooking process.

Technique
    A small amount of butter is heated in a heavy skillet. Thin and delicate fillets are usually floured or breaded before they are cooked to help protect their flesh while thicker steaks are generally fried as they are. When the pan is hot add the fish and sprinkle the filets with salt and pepper. Turn the fish once during the cooking time using a long handled turner that will support the weight of the fish. Filets will need to be cooked 2-3 minutes a side while thick steaks will need 4-5 minutes per side. The fish are cooked until their flesh flakes and they lose their translucency.

    At this point the fish can be served as it is or a sauce can be added. To do this remove the fish to a heated platter and add a few tablespoons of butter and lemon juice. Place the pan back on the heat for the butter to melt and mingle with the lemon and pan juices. After the liquids have been whisked about with a fork they are poured over the cooked fish and fresh parsley is sprinkled over all. This cooking method is called "meunière" which means in French "the way of the miller's wife." If you have never cooked fish before try one of the following fish cooked meunière style.

Sauté the Following Fish and Shellfish:

Abalone	Perch	Shrimp
Albacore	Petrale Sole	Skate
Clams	Rex Sole	Smelt
Crab	Sablefish	Snapper
Dover Sole	Salmon	Steelhead
English	Sanddabs	Sturgeon
Halibut	Scallops	Swordfish
Lingcod	Sea Bass	Trout
Oysters	Shark	True Cod
Pacific Flounder		

BAKING

Most fish can be baked successfully. The delicate textured fillets, such as the soles, can be breaded and baked, or sauced and baked, at 400 degrees until they are done. The sauce or breading protects the fillets from the heat. Fish that have a firmer structure, such as salmon, steelhead, snapper, sea bass, black cod, halibut, albacore, swordfish, lingcod and true cod, can be baked as they are at 350 degrees until they are done.

Technique

Butter a baking dish large enough to hold the fish fillets or steaks. Season the fish with salt and pepper and place a slice of onion, a slice of lemon and 1/2 teaspoon of butter on each fish fillet or steak. Cover the pan with foil or with a lid and bake at the required temperature (see previous paragraph) until the fish is done. There is no need to turn the fish. If you are baking a whole fish you will first need to determine how long it should bake. Lay the fish on a flat surface. Hold a ruler perpendicular to the back of the fish and measure the thickness of the fish. It will need to bake 10 minutes for every inch of thickness. (This same method can be used to determine the length of time to cook thick fish steaks.) Place it in a large baking dish or roasting pan. Place three slices each of onion and lemon inside the cavity and sprinkle with salt and pepper. Cover the dish with foil and bake it at 450 degrees until the fish is done.

Bake the Following Fish and Shellfish:

Albacore	Perch	Shark
Abalone	Petrale Sole	Skate
Crab	Rex Sole	Snapper
English Sole	Sablefish	Steelhead
Halibut	Salmon	Sturgeon
Lingcod	Sanddabs	Swordfish
Mackerel	Scallops	Trout
Pacific Flounder	Sea Bass	Turbot

BROILING

Firm fleshed fish and those with medium to high fat content can all be broiled successfully either as steaks or as fillets.

Technique

Preheat the oven to broil. Move the top oven rack so that the broiler pan will be four inches from the coils. Place the fish on the broiling pan, season with salt and pepper and brush with melted butter. Place the pan in the oven leaving the oven door partly ajar. Broil using the ten minute rule. Brush the fish with melted butter after turning.

Broil the Following Fish:

Albacore	Rex Sole	Steelhead
Flounder	Sablefish	Sturgeon
Halibut	Salmon	Swordfish
Lingcod	Sanddabs	Trout
Mackerel	Shark	True Cod
Petrale Sole	Snapper	Turbot

GRILLING

Firm fleshed fish with medium to high fat content are all

excellent grilled. This is my favorite method for cooking these fish. They can be grilled either as steaks or as fillets.

Technique

Start the barbecue, using either charcoal or mesquite. (Mesquite is a type of hardwood that is becoming more and more popular in the United States because it burns very hot and therefore cooks food quickly.)

Make the lemon-butter sauce below. If you are cooking steaks place them on the grill and brush them with the lemon-butter. Cook them 4 minutes per side. Brush them with the melted butter once they are turned. When they are done place on a warmed platter and brush them once again with the lemon butter. Serve immediately garnished with fresh parsley.

If you are cooking a large fish fillet, place it on the grill flesh side down. Cook it for 15 minutes, turn the fish over and ladle the lemon-butter sauce with the onions onto the flesh. Cook for 10 more minutes or until the fish flakes with a fork.

LEMON-BUTTER SAUCE

8 tablespoons butter
1 onion, chopped
1/4 cup chopped parsley
Juice of 1 lemon
3/4 teaspoon fresh tarragon, minced
or
1/2 teaspoon whole tarragon, crushed

Place all the ingredients in a small sauce pan and cook over low heat until the onions are tender, about 20 minutes.

Grill the Following Fish and Shellfish:

Albacore	Salmon	Swordfish
Halibut	Shark	Trout
Mackerel	Steelhead	True Cod
Sablefish	Sturgeon	

Easy and Elegant Seafood

POACHING

Poaching is a method of cooking food in a small amount of simmering liquid. Almost all fish and shellfish can be poached successfully.

Technique

If you want to poach fillets or steaks you will need a skillet with a lid that is at least 2 inches deep or, if you plan on poaching them in the oven, an oven-proof baking dish. Add 1/4 cup dry white wine and 3/4 cup water to the pan. There should be about 1/4 inch of water in the bottom of the pan. Place a tight fitting lid on the pan and bring the liquid to a boil.

Sprinkle the flesh with salt and pepper and place a slice each of onion and lemon on top of each piece. Reduce the heat and place the fish in the poaching liquid. Simmer until they are done. Fillets will need about 8-10 minutes, and steaks 10-15 minutes. If you want to poach the fish in the oven, turn the oven to 400 degrees and cook the fillets for 12-15 minutes and steaks for 18-22 minutes.

The best way to poach a whole fish is in a poaching pan. If you do not have one a roasting pan will work. If you do not have either one of those, cut the fish in half and use two deep skillets or baking dishes if you plan on poaching the fish in the oven. Prepare the poaching liquid or court bouillon by placing the following ingredients in the poaching pan:

- 3 quarts water
- 3 cups dry white wine
- 1 onion, peeled and quartered
- 2 cloves of garlic, crushed
- 20 whole peppercorns
- 1 tablespoon salt
- 1 sliced lemon
- 1 teaspoon whole thyme, crushed
- 1 bay leaf, broken in two

Bring the poaching ingredients to a boil and simmer for 1 hour. Measure the thickness of the fish with a ruler to determine how long it will take to cook the fish. You will need to cook the fish 8-10 minutes for every inch of thickness. The head and tail can be removed or left attached. Wrap the fish in cheesecloth, place it in the poaching liquid and cover the pan. Bring the liquid to a boil then turn the heat to simmer. Turn the fish halfway through the cooking time.

Poach the Following Fish and Shellfish:

Albacore	Scallops	Sturgeon
Halibut	Shark	Swordfish
Lingcod	Shrimp	Trout
Oysters	Snapper	True Cod
Salmon	Steelhead	

Poach the Following Whole Fish:

| Salmon | Steelhead |

STEAMING
An alternative to poaching is steaming. Any type of fish can be steamed but those with the most delicate flesh, such as the soles, are excellent cooked in this manner. Steam either filets or steaks.

Technique

Lay the fish in the top half of a vegetable steamer. Pour a small amount of water in the bottom half and place the fish over it. Steam the fillets or steaks using the 10 minute rule.

MICROWAVE
Pieces of fish that are all the same thickness, such as steaks, can be cooked in the microwave with great success. Place the fish in a glass baking dish and season with salt and pepper. Lay a lemon slice, a piece of onion and a teaspoon of butter on top of each steak. Cover the dish with plastic wrap and microwave on high 4 minutes per pound. At the end of the cooking time, if the fish does not look cooked in the center, let it stand covered for several more minutes and the internal heat will complete the cooking process.

Microwave the Following Fish:

Albacore	Perch	Sturgeon
Halibut	Sablefish	Swordfish
Lingcod	Salmon	True Cod
Pacific Snapper	Steelhead	

Some Fishy Information

Listed below are brief descriptive sketches of some of the most popular culinary fish and shellfish in the United States today.

ALBACORE
Albacore is one of six species of tuna which is a member of the mackerel family. It is the only tuna whose flesh is canned and sold as "white meat." Normally these fish prefer to remain in deeper waters but with the changing El Niño current in the Pacific Ocean they have been coming closer to shore to look for food. Consequently, we are seeing more fresh albacore in the fish markets than usual.

How to Cook
Sauté, bake, broil, grill, poach, microwave.

How to Buy
Albacore is usually sold as loins.

    4-6 ounces per person
    8-12 ounces for 2 people
    1-1/2 - 2 pounds for 4 people

CRAB
There are more than 4,500 species of crab. In the United States there are only five crabs of commercial importance: the stone crab and blue crab from the Atlantic Ocean and the king, snow, and Dungeness crabs of the West Coast. The blue crab or softshell crab is distinguished from the other four crustaceans because its last pair of legs is flat which enables it to swim. It is also one of the only crabs that is mar-

keted after it molts and before its new shell becomes hard; it is consumed shell and all.

The Dungeness crab, harvested from northern California to the Aleutian Islands, is fished in Alaska in the summer months and from Alaska southward in the winter months. Out of the three states of Washington, Oregon and California, Oregon provides one-third of the total catch of Dungeness crab. Over 98% of the crabs are taken from the Oregon Coast while the other 2% comes from coastal bays. The bays tend to act as a nursery for the young crabs but as they mature they tend to migrate in a non-specific pattern along the coast.

A Dungeness crab is mature at three years of age and its shell width must be a minimum of six to seven inches before it can be taken from the ocean or bay by commercial or non-commercial fishermen. Only male crabs are harvested because the female is generally smaller than the male with not much useable meat.

There are three species of king crab: the red king, blue king and golden king; all are members of the stone crab family. The king crab is one of Alaska's most valuable fishing industries. The backmeat of the king crab is generally canned while the legs are frozen and sold in the shell.

How to Buy

Crab can be purchased in several different forms: live, cooked in the shell and picked. Whole Dungeness crab are sold by the crab, cooked or live. One crab will serve approximately 2 - 3 people. When you buy whole cooked crab in the fish market it should be bright reddish-orange and it should not have an unpleasant odor. It will also save you time and trouble if you ask to have it cleaned. Crab is also sold shelled by the pound. Picked legs are more expensive than picked crab back with assorted pieces. One pound of picked crab meat is about 2 cups. Only the legs of the Alaskan king crab are usually sold.

Best Method for Cooking:

The Oregon Department of Fish and Wildlife recommends that you remove the back of the crab before cooking. After the back is removed, break the crab in two, shake the viscera out and remove the gills. Add 3 to 5 ounces of salt to a gallon of water and bring it to a boil. Add the crabs and when the water starts to boil again, cook for 12-15 minutes. Remove the crabs and immerse them in cold water to stop the cooking process. The cold water also prevents shrinkage of the meat and helps to keep the meat from adhering to the shell.

Crab can be reheated by steaming or microwaving. A piece of crab backmeat microwaved on high for 20 seconds will be hot throughout.

CLAMS

There are more than 20,000 species of clams found the world over in both salt and fresh water buried in either mud or sand. All clams are vegetarians that strain algae from the water. Although they reach maturity between 1 and 3 years of age, some live to be 20 years old.

Clams have been a valuable source of food to mankind and in North America their shells were used to make wampum. The American Indians took the purple and white parts of the Quahog clam and drilled holes in it. It was then strung to make belts and other decorative items that were used in trading.

RAZOR CLAMS. The West Coast and East Coast each have their own species of razor clam. The razor clam of the East Coast is long and slender with square ends. It resembles the straight edge of an old-fashioned razor and thus the name "razor clam." The razor clam on the West Coast is much shorter and wider than its distant East Coast cousin and it has rounded ends. Both of these clams have shells with razor sharp edges that can quickly cut your fingers when you are digging for them.

The scientific name for the razor clam is *Siqua patula* which means "spreading foot," referring to its foot which expands when it takes in water so that it can act as an anchor. This foot or digger also provides the clam with a means to rapidly pull itself downward through the sand. It can dig vertically as fast as 1 to 2 feet per minute!

The razor clam is one of the few clams on the West Coast that is found in open sandy beaches at low tides; the butter clam, horseneck clam and geoduck clam all reside in bays. If you have ever gone clamming you will understand the feeling of frustration when trying to dig these elusive creatures while simultaneously trying to avoid getting drenched by an unsuspecting wave.

If you choose to dig your own clams instead of buying them at the fish market, you will need to know how to clean these bivalves. Remove the clam from the shell by running the blade of a sharp knife down the inside of the clam near the hinge to cut the two abductor muscles. Remove the clam and cut off the tip of the neck. Split the neck its entire length with a pair of scissors. Remove the dark portions or gills and then rinse the clams under running cold water.

Some people like to remove the neck and mince it for chowder because it tends to be tough. I generally leave it attached to the clam and cook it anyway. It is somewhat tough but it has a good flavor.

Best Cooking Methods
Sauté.

How to Buy
Razor clams are sold out of the shells ready to be cooked. The meat should look creamy-white and glistening. There are about 15-20 razor clams in a pound.

>3-4 clams per person
>6-8 clams for 2 people
>12-16 clams for 4 people

LITTLENECK CLAMS. There are two species of littleneck clams found on the West Coast: the native littleneck and the Japanese littleneck. They can be found in bays and beaches with rocky shores and they are also called steamer or butter clams. They are small, resembling a cockle and measure about 1-2 inches long from the hinge to the front of the shell. There are about 12-15 clams in a pound.

Best Cooking Methods

Steam or cook at the last minute in fish soups such as cioppino or bouillabaisse.

How to Buy

These clams are generally bought live and their shells should be tightly closed. They are also sold frozen in their shells and shucked. There are about 12 - 15 clams in a pound.

    8 ounces of steamer clams per person
    1 pound of steamer clams for 2 people
    2 pounds of steamer clams for 4 people

BUTTER CLAMS. The butter clam is also called a Quahog, Beefsteak, Washington, Coney Island or Great Oregon clam. Their average size is 2-3 inches from the hinge to the front of the shell and they live in the gravel and mud-sand bottoms of bays.

Best Cooking Methods

Many people consider these clams the best clams for making clam chowder.

How to Buy

This species of clam is not commonly found in fish markets. It is usually minced and canned commercially.

HORSENECK CLAMS. The horseneck clam is also called the gaper, horse, blue or empire clam. It is a bay clam that prefers sand or sand-mud.

Best Cooking Method

Mince for chowders and fritters. The siphon can be dipped in boiling water before peeling the rough outer layer of skin.

How to Buy

This clam is not commonly found in fish markets.

GEODUCK. The geoduck is the largest clam in the United States and it is found in British Columbia and Washington

State. The name geoduck comes from the Nisqually Indians and means "dig deep." Noted in the Educational Bulletin put out by the Fish Commission of Oregon was a geoduck that was dug in May of 1949 that weighed 6½ pounds and its shell length measured 6¾ inches! This strange looking bivalve has a rectangular shell and its body is so large that it hangs out at both ends. The meat of the geoduck has an excellent flavor which tends to be a little on the sweet side.

How to Cook
Remove the clam from its shell by cutting the abductor muscles. Remove the siphon and dip it in boiling water before peeling the rough outer layer of skin. Clean the clam by removing the innards. It can now be run through the coarse blade of a meat grinder or chopped for 30 seconds in a food processor and used for chowders. Cut the clam into thin slices for frying or it can be eaten uncooked in a marinade.

How to Buy
This clam is usually sold with most of it in its shell. The average weight of this clam and its shell is 3 pounds which will yield 1½ pounds of edible meat.

1 clam serves 2-3 people.

COD
There are 75 species of cods; only two of the species are found in fresh water. The Pacific cod is one of three species found in the Pacific Ocean of North America. It is also known as true cod or gray cod (in British Columbia). The market term for this fish in the Pacific Northwest is "true cod." Since it is closely related to the Atlantic cod, their recipes are interchangeable.

The largest known "true cod" weighed 211 pounds.

Best Cooking Methods
Sauté, bake, broil, grill, poach, steam, microwave.

How to Buy
Cod is usually sold as a fillet.

4 - 6 ounces per person
8 - 12 ounces for 2 people
1 - 1-1/2 pounds for 4 people

CRAYFISH

Crayfish are also called crawdads or crawdaddies and they have changed very little over the last million years. There are more than 300 different species and North America alone has more than 250 species and subspecies.

Fortunately for those who enjoy eating these tasty critters commercial farming of crayfish is becoming a big industry in the United States. Louisiana is the leading producer with over 90% of the nation's crayfish being raised in that state.

Live crayfish can be stored at 40 degrees for up to three days if there is good air circulation. Clean them before cooking by pulling the middle tail flipper straight out and the intestine will be attached to it. Once cooked, the meat in the claws and the tail are considered by most to be the edible delicacies of these crustaceans.

Best Method for Cooking
Boil in salted water for 3 to 5 minutes.

How to Buy
There are about 8 crayfish in a pound.

1-1/2 pounds per person
3 pounds for 2 people
6 pounds for 4 people

FLATFISH

This group of fish is found world-wide and contains more than 600 species. Included are many of our most common table fish: flounder, turbot, halibut, petrale sole, Dover sole, rex sole, English sole and sanddabs. The two most important flounders commercially in the United States are the yellowtail flounder and the winter flounder, both found off the East Coast.

There are no true soles from the family Soleidae found in the United States. Authentic sole comes from the coastal regions near France and England. The fish that we call sole are actually members of the flounder family.

ENGLISH SOLE is a small flounder with a very mild flavor and a delicate texture. It is sometimes called lemon sole.

Best Method for Cooking
   Sauté, bake, broil, poach.

How to Buy
   It is marketed as a fillet. You will need 1-1/2 pounds to serve four people.

   4 - 6 ounces per person
   8 - 12 ounces for 2 people
   1 to 1-1/2 pounds for 4 people

DOVER SOLE* is a Pacific flounder with a mild flavor and texture. It is most commonly marketed as "fillet of sole" and is the most plentiful of the members of this family. *It is also the name of the common sole of Europe (*Solea vulgaris*).

Best Method for Cooking
   Sauté, bake, broil, steam.

How to Buy
   It is marketed as a fillet.

   4 - 6 ounces per person
   8 - 12 ounces for 2 people
   1 to 1-1/2 pounds for 4 people

PETRALE SOLE is a large Pacific flounder that is ranked "number one" for the best flavor and texture of all the soles.

Best Method for Cooking
   Sauté, bake, broil, poach, steam.

How to Buy
   It is marketed as a fillet.

4 - 6 ounces per person
8 - 12 ounces for 2 people
1 to 1-1/2 pounds for 4 people

REX SOLE is a small Pacific flounder that has a good flavor and a delicate texture. It has a bony plate in the center that is easily removed once the fish is cooked.

Best Method for Cooking
Sauté, bake, broil, poach.

How to Buy
Rex sole is usually pan-dressed and ready to be cooked.

4 - 6 ounces per person
8 - 12 ounces for 2 people
1 to 1-1/2 pounds for 4 people

TURBOT is a Pacific flounder that has a mild flavor and a delicate texture.

Best Method for Cooking
Sauté, bake, broil, poach.

How to Buy
Turbot is usually sold as fillets.

4 - 6 ounces per person
8 - 12 ounces for 2 people
1 to 1-1/2 pounds for 4 people

HALIBUT is a flounder that has firm, dense, white flesh with a delicate flavor. It is the largest flatfish found off the Pacific Coast. A female can weigh over 500 pounds!

Best Method for Cooking
Broil, grill, sauté, bake, microwave.

How to Buy
Halibut is usually sold in thick 1 inch steaks.

6 - 8 ounces per person
1 pound for 2 people
2 pounds for 4 people

The **SANDDAB** is also a flounder found in both the Atlantic and Pacific oceans. It has a mild flavor, a delicate texture and a bony plate that is easily removed after cooking.

Best Method for Cooking
Sauté, bake, broil, poach.

How to Buy
Sanddabs are usually sold whole and pan-dressed.

4 - 6 ounces per person
8 - 12 ounces for 2 people
1 to 1-1/2 ounces for 4 people

LINGCOD
The lingcod is one of nine species of the greenling family found in North America from Kodiak, Alaska, to Baja, Mexico. Lingcod are highly prized both as sport fish and as valuable commercial fish. It has a delicate flavor and firm, but tender, flesh. With their looks they would never win a beauty contest but at a fish tasting contest they would receive top marks for texture and flavor.

Best Cooking Methods
Sauté, poach, broil, bake, grill, microwave.

How to Buy
Lingcod is sold as fillets or steaks.

4 - 6 ounces per person
8 - 12 ounces for 2 people
1 to 1-1/2 pounds for 4 people

MUSSELS
The California mussel is found from Alaska to Mexico attached to rocks and pilings in the ocean and in coastal bays.

Its flesh is bright orange which creates a dramatic and eye-appealing contrast with its black shells. The blue or edible mussel is found in Europe and along the East Coast as far south as North Carolina. It has a blue-black shell and white flesh. Both mussels can often be found in fish markets. The difference in taste between the two is negligible.

If you are going to gather your own mussels, always try to pick those which are about 2 inches long. Their flavor is superior to extra large mussels.

Best Method for Cooking

Sauté, steam, bake or poach. If you have bought or gathered mussels that still have the beard attached, cut off as much as possible with scissors and scrub the shell with a small brush. The rest of the beard can be removed from the mussel with a gentle tug after it is cooked. Mussels can be removed from their shells by steaming, baking or by microwaving on medium-high for 30 seconds.

How to Buy

Mussels are bought live and their shell should be completely closed. There are about 10 medium-sized mussels in a pound.

- 1 pound per person
- 2 pounds for 2 people
- 4 pounds for 4 people

SMOKED MUSSELS are a new item in the fish markets. They are already cooked and sold out of their shells.

Best Method for Cooking

Use them in soups, marinated in salads or just eat them with herb mayonnaise.

How to Buy

There are about 15 - 20 smoked mussels per pound.

12 ounces serves 4 as an appetizer.

OYSTERS

Throughout the world there are ten species of oysters of culinary importance, four of them from North America.

The two main species of oysters found in the Pacific Northwest are the Olympia and the Pacific. The tiny Olympia oyster, indigenous to Washington State, is also called the Willapa oyster because in the late 1800s it was heavily harvested from Willapa Bay and Puget Sound.

Over 13 million pounds of oysters are harvested from the coastal waters of California, Oregon, Washington, British Columbia and Alaska. Washington is the leading producer of oysters with over 85% of the total harvest.

Over-harvesting and water pollution have seriously endangered this species and fortunately the native oyster has been saved from extinction by oyster culturing. The center for the oyster culture industry is near Olympia, Washington, and therefore the name "Olympia oyster." Luckily this oyster has always managed to reseed itself; there are no other oysters of this species anywhere in the world.

The second species of oyster found in the Pacific Northwest is the Pacific oyster which was introduced from Japan in 1905. We now have a flourishing oyster industry thanks to the foresight of the United States Commissioner of Fisheries who, in 1889, recommended that the Japanese oyster seed be transplanted to the coastal regions of the West Coast. It has adapted well to our coast and it is the number one oyster harvested for commercial purposes on the West Coast. It is much larger than the tiny, native Olympia oyster and it can be bought in varying sizes which are set by the Pacific Coast Oyster Growers Association. The oysters are sold in pint jars labeled large (8 oysters to a jar), medium (9 - 12 oysters per jar), small (13 - 18 oysters per jar), and extra small (19 or more oysters per jar). In case you haven't noticed, the retail price of oysters is inversely proportional to the size of the oyster: the smaller the oyster the higher the price! This is a subtle indication that the smaller the oysters the greater the delicacy.

Best Method for Cooking

Sauté, bake (fresh oysters are delicious raw on the half shell).

How to Buy

1/2 pint jar (medium) per person
1 pint jar (medium) for two people
1-1/2 to 2 pint jars (medium) for 4 people

ROCKFISH

There are more than 100 species of rockfish and most of them can be found in the Pacific Ocean. There are five species, however, that are found in the North Atlantic and one in the South Atlantic where they are called redfishes.

Two common rockfish are the red rockfish, most commonly called Pacific snapper and the Pacific Ocean perch.

PACIFIC SNAPPER. This fish has a mild flavor with finely-textured flesh.

Best Cooking Methods
Sauté, bake, poach, broil, grill, microwave.

How to Buy
Fillets.

4 - 6 ounces per person
8 - 12 ounces for 2 people
1 to 1-1/2 pounds for 4 people

PERCH. The most important commercial rockfish on the Pacific Coast is the perch. It is mild tasting with medium-firm flesh.

Best Cooking Methods
Sauté, bake, poach, broil, grill, microwave.

How to Buy
Fillets.

4 - 6 ounces per person
8 - 12 ounces for two people
1 to 1-1/2 pounds for 4 people

SABLEFISH

Sablefish is often incorrectly called black cod. There are only two species of this fish and both of them are found in the Pacific. It has a widespread distribution ranging from Japan and the Bering Sea to central Baja. It has a pleasant flavor, delicate texture and is high in fish oils; consequently, it is delicious smoked.

Best Cooking Methods
Sauté, bake, broil, grill, smoke, microwave.

How to Buy
Sablefish is sold most commonly as steaks or fillets. It is also sold as roasts or pan-dressed (head and viscera removed).

  4 - 5 ounces per person
  8 - 12 ounces for 2 people
  1 to 1-1/2 pounds for 4 people

SCALLOPS

There are more than 400 different species of scallops. They are different than most bivalves because they are capable of being free-swimming. They do not travel great distances but they move about within the bed by expelling water through their shells, which the Shell Oil Company has made famous.

The East Coast scallop industry is more than a hundred years old, whereas West Coast fishermen did not start to fish for scallops until the late 1960s. Alaskan waters provided beds of weathervane scallops but it was soon realized that dredging the beds was destroying the king crab. In 1969 the Alaska legislature closed scallop harvesting permanently to protect the king crab.

The weathervane scallop is found from central California to Alaska. In 1981, beds of this scallop were discovered off the coast of Oregon by two East Coast scallop dredgers who had left Alaskan waters. A bed near Coos Bay has been estimated to have more than 11 million pounds of scallops. Scallops reach a commercially harvestable size when they are seven years old. It is too early to tell if, after a heavy harvest, there will be adequate conditions for spawning of this newly discovered scallop.

Best Cooking Methods
Sauté, poach, bake.

How to Buy
Scallops are sold already removed from their shell. There are about 200 bay scallops per pound and about 30 to 40 sea scallops per pound.

> 5 ounces of scallops per person
> 10 ounces of scallops for 2 people
> 1-1/4 pound scallops for 4 people

SHRIMP
The United States commercially produces seven species of shrimp from the Atlantic Coast and the Gulf of Mexico and five from the West Coast. The major shrimp producing area on the West Coast is Kodiak, Alaska, where *Pandalus borealis*, a small pink shrimp, is the major shrimp harvested. Another shrimp, *Pandalus jordani*, is the second species of small pink shrimp trawled on the West Coast from California to Vancouver Island.

There are three species of large shrimp found on the West Coast and they are marketed as prawns. Their body sizes range from 4 to 6 inches, much larger than the bodies of the small pink shrimp which are only 3 to 5 inches long. The only part of both the large and small shrimp that is usually eaten is the tail.

Best Cooking Method
Both large and small shrimp are usually sold in fish markets already cooked although some large shrimp are sold uncooked or "green." If you have gathered your own shrimp the best method for cooking is to steam them.

How to Buy
There are 2 cups of small pink shrimp in a pound, 35 - 40 small prawns to a pound, 20 - 25 medium prawns to a pound

and 16 - 20 large prawns to a pound.

    4 - 6 ounces of medium-sized prawns per serving
    8 - 12 ounces of medium-sized prawns for 2
    1 to 1-1/2 pounds medium-sized prawns for 4

SALMON

Salmon are members of a large group of fish that inhabited the seas over 135 million years ago while dinosaurs were still roaming the land. After millions of years they evolved into the family, Salmonidae, which includes both salmon and trout. Both of these species require the cold waters of the Northern Hemisphere.

Many scientists speculate that the Pacific salmon is a distant relative of the Atlantic salmon. In between Ice Ages, five hundred thousand to a million years ago, a group of adventurous Atlantic salmon traveled north, possibly through the Arctic Ocean and the Bering Sea, to reach the Pacific Ocean. (Another theory suggests that they reached the Pacific Ocean by a fresh-water route.) In either case, once they arrived in the Pacific Ocean they decided to stay and began to adapt to their new environment. During the process of evolution, Pacific salmon gradually evolved into six separate species.

We have five species of salmon in the Pacific Northwest. The sixth species, the Cherry salmon, is found only in Asia.

All five species are anadromous which means that they hatch from eggs in fresh water but travel to the ocean to spend the next two to eight years. When they are mature they will return to the stream in which they were born to spawn and then to die. Some fish, like the chinook salmon, have been known to travel up to a thousand miles in the river part of their migration.

CHINOOK SALMON. The chinook salmon, also commonly called king salmon, or spring salmon, is the largest member of the Pacific salmon family and it is the finest tasting of all the species. When caught, either in the ocean or not far from the ocean, its flesh is a bright red color. This bright color begins to fade when the salmon start fasting while they journey up the river to spawn. The chinook has the highest fat content of the five Pacific salmon and consequently when it is cooked the meat has large flakes with a soft texture.

CHINOOK SALMON (WHITE). The white chinook or king salmon can occasionally be found in fish markets labeled "white king." It is a rare strain of chinook salmon that has white meat instead of the characteristic reddish-orange. For some unknown reason it does not assimilate the pigment, astaxanthin, found in many crustaceans that salmon feed on. This unusual salmon is excellent to eat and some consider it to be the best tasting of all the salmon species.

COHO SALMON. The coho salmon is also called a silver salmon. It is smaller than the chinook salmon but is almost equally delicious. It contains half the amount of fat as the chinook and has large, tender, firm flakes of meat.

SOCKEYE SALMON. The sockeye salmon is often called the red salmon or the blueback salmon. It is easily recognizable because of its bright red flesh. It has a higher fat content than the coho but not quite as high as the chinook. It has tender, large flakes and the flavor is comparable to either the coho or the chinook. Due to its high fat content, it commands an equally high price as the chinook. It is highly prized for canning. The landlocked form of this fish is called a kokanee.

CHUM SALMON. This salmon is also called the dog or fall salmon. The chum salmon has the palest color of meat of the five species. It is almost flesh colored, has the lowest fat content and tends to have the least amount of flavor. It is often sold canned or smoked.

PINK SALMON. The pink salmon, the smallest of the salmon species, is also called the humpback salmon. It is the most abundant of all the species although it is seldom sold in fish markets. Commercially it is most often processed in cans.

Best Cooking Methods
Sauté, broil, grill, bake, poach, microwave.

How to Buy
Salmon is sold as steaks, as fillets, or whole.

Steaks:
One 6 - 8 ounce steak per person
Two 6 - 8 ounce steaks for two people
Four 6 - 8 ounce steaks for four people

Fillets:
4 - 6 ounces per person
8 - 12 ounces for 2 people
1 to 1-1/2 pounds for 4 people

Whole:
Plan on serving 1/2 pound salmon per person. A whole salmon will lose about 1-1/2 pounds when the head, tail and bones are removed.

Example:
To serve a whole salmon to 20 dinner guests you will need 10 pounds of salmon. Add 1½ pounds (loss from head, tail and bones) to the 10 pounds and you will need to order a 11½-pound salmon to serve 20 people.

SKATE

Skates and sharks are both members of the same class, Chondrichthyes, which are the cartilaginous fish. The skate is a flat, wide, scaleless fish with fins in the form of wings. It travels about in the water by moving its wings in an undulating motion. This wing is the edible portion of the skate. It has a firm, white meat very similar to the sea scallop. It is so similar, in fact, that meat taken from the skate wing is sometimes used in less reputable restaurants in place of sea scallops.

It is difficult to get excited about eating skate when you see their unappetizing wings. Do not let the skate's appearance stop you from purchasing this delicious fish. It is one of the least expensive items in the fish market and you will be pleasantly surprised by its wonderful flavor.

Best Cooking Methods
Sauté, bake, poach.

How to Buy
Only the tips of the wings are sold and they will be rectangular strips.

> 8 ounces per person
> 1 pound for 2 people
> 2 pounds for 4 people

STURGEON

The sturgeon is the largest fresh-water fish in the United States. It is also the fresh-water fish with the greatest longevity, with many living to be over 75 years of age!

There are 16 sturgeon species found in the world today. The United States has 7 species with 2 species found in the Pacific Northwest — the green sturgeon and white (or Pacific) sturgeon. The white sturgeon is the most highly prized for its meat and it is usually sold fresh as fillets or smoked. The green sturgeon is marketed as a smoked, canned product.

Sturgeon are now being raised on commercial aquaculture farms thanks to the work of Wally Clark and Sergei Doroshov. Mr. Doroshov, who defected from Russia, is a fish biologist who specializes in sturegeons. The two scientists began their program at the University of California at Davis three years ago and have been very successful.

Best Cooking Methods
Sauté, bake, broil, poach, grill, smoke, microwave.

How to Buy
Sturgeon do not have bones but a notocord instead, which is removed before the fish is marketed. Sturgeon is available in fish markets as fillets or steaks.

6 - 8 ounces per person
1 pound for 2 people
2 pounds for 4 people

SWORDFISH

There is only one species of swordfish, *Xiphias gladius*. Its scientific name aptly describes this unique fish since xiphias is a Greek word meaning sword-shaped and gladius is the Latin name for a type of sword used during ancient Roman times.

The habitat of this fish is worldwide in tropical or temperate waters. On the West Coast it is found from Oregon southward.

It has excellent flavor and firm flesh.

Best Cooking Methods

Sauté, bake, broil, poach, grill, microwave.

How to Buy

Swordfish is usually sold as steaks.

1/2 pound per person
1 pound for 2 people
2 pounds for 4 people

TROUT/STEELHEAD

Universally, trout are the most cultured fish raised for commercial purposes and angling. There are many species of this fish and each has its own distinct flavor. My favorite trout to eat is the steelhead, which is also called a "sea-run rainbow trout." It is a rainbow trout that spends part of its life in the ocean and inhabits the Pacific Ocean from Alaska to central California to Japan and the Bering Sea. Like salmon, the steelhead is an anadromous fish, meaning that it leaves the river and returns to its natal river to spawn. It spawns in coastal streams in the winter and spring and the young remain there for two to three years. Then they migrate to the ocean for two to three years and travel extensively. Unlike salmon, all steelhead do not die after spawning; many return to the ocean but only a tiny percentage survive a second spawning.

Some Fishy Information

The flesh of the steelhead just after it has started up the river to spawn is bright orange, similar to a chinook salmon. Once it starts on its long journey upriver it starts to fast and the bright color gradually fades to a pale white.

Steelhead, with its moist and succulent flesh, is one of my favorite fish to eat. I prefer it grilled with onions and lemon butter (see page 129). Its flavor is the best when it is just starting up the river to spawn.

Best Cooking Method
Sauté, bake, poach, barbecue, broil, smoke, microwave.

How to Buy
It is illegal to sell steelhead in most states. If you have caught your own or have had one given to you it can be cooked whole or cut into fillets or steaks.

> 6 - 8 ounces per person
> 1 pound for 2 people
> 2 pounds for 4 people

Appetizers

ANTIPASTO BASKET WITH HERB MAYONNAISE
(Serves 4)

This is probably my favorite of all appetizers. It is simple to prepare, tastes delicious and makes a beautiful presentation. It can be served in either a basket or on a platter or plate. Line the one you choose with crisp lettuce leaves.

- 3 large carrots, peeled and cut into 1/2 x 2-1/2 inch lengths
- 3 large stalks of celery, cut into 1/2 x 2-1/2 inch lengths
- 12 cherry tomatoes
- 8 midget sweet pickles
- 1 3-1/4 ounce can pitted black olives
- 1 pound prawns, cooked and peeled (see page 35)
- 1/2 pound smoked mussels or 1 can smoked oysters
- 1 English cucumber, cut into 1/2 x 2-1/2 inch lengths
- 1 red bell pepper, seeded and cut into 1/2 x 2-1/2 inch lengths
- 7 or 8 crisp lettuce leaves, washed
- 4 thinly sliced lemons
- 4 sprigs of fresh parsley

Arrange the lettuce leaves in a circular pattern covering the bottom of the basket. Arrange all of the above items decoratively on the lettuce leaving room for the bowl of herb mayonnaise in the center of the dish. Garnish the platter with the lemons and sprigs of fresh parsley. Photo page 65.

Appetizers

HERB MAYONNAISE

1 whole egg
1 teaspoon wine vinegar
1/2 teaspoon salt
1 clove garlic, peeled
3 tablespoons parsley
3 tablespoons scallions
1-1/2 cups mild olive oil

Place the egg, vinegar, salt, garlic, parsley, and scallions in the bowl of a food processor or blender and blend for 30 seconds. With the machine still running, slowly add the oil and the mixture will gradually thicken.

Put the herb mayonnaise in a small bowl and set it in the middle of the basket.

CURRIED TUNA

This recipe is the creation of a special friend, Karen Sehon, who lives in Redding, California. She serves the curried tuna as a spread for crisp crackers or for sandwiches served on whole grain breads.

1 6-1/2 ounce can tuna, packed in oil, drained
5 tablespoons of mayonnaise
4 green onions, thinly sliced including the green end
1/8 cup raw almonds, chopped finely
1/2 cup raisins
1 teaspoon curry powder
1 teaspoon mustard

Mix the tuna with the mayonnaise, curry and mustard. Add the other ingredients and blend well. Let the curried tuna sit for several hours for their flavors to meld.

CLAMS STUFFED WITH DUNGENESS CRAB AND CREAM CHEESE (Serves 4)

East meets West in this recipe: cherrystone clams, popular on the East Coast, are stuffed with the popular West Coast Dungeness crab, cream cheese and lemon thyme.

4 cherrystone clams
1/2 pound shelled crab meat
1-1/2 ounces cream cheese
3 green onions, chopped
1/2 teaspoon fresh lemon thyme, chopped or scant 1/4 teaspoon dried thyme
Salt and pepper to taste

Preheat the oven to 400 degrees.
Place the clams in a small pan with a lid. Add enough water to cover the bottom of the pan and cover with the lid. Turn the heat to high and cook the clams until they pop open, about 4 - 5 minutes. Let the clams cool.
Remove the clams from their shells and coarsely chop the meat with a sharp knife. Mix the chopped clams with the rest of the ingredients. Place a heaping tablespoon of this mixture back into each shell half. Heat the stuffed clams for 10 minutes or until the cream cheese melts.
Serve each person 2 stuffed clam halves accompanied with a cocktail fork.

Microwave technique: Place the clams in the microwave for 45 seconds on high or until they pop open. Follow the above instructions. Heat the stuffed clams in the microwave for 30 seconds on high until the cream cheese melts.

Variation: Substitute 1 pound of steamer clams for the cherrystone clams. Follow the above instructions except add 1 teaspoon of filling to each shell half. Serve each person 6 - 8 stuffed clam halves accompanied with a cocktail fork. Photo page 66.

HUMBOLDT COUNTY CLAM DIP (Serves 4 - 6)

I grew up in Humboldt County, a small lumber and fishing community situated on the Pacific Coast about 300 miles north of San Francisco. Seafood and shellfish were always plentiful and this dip was usually present during festive occasions. It tastes best if it is made a day ahead but it can be served immediately.

1 8 ounce package of cream cheese
1 6-1/2 ounce can minced clams, drained but reserve the juice
1 small onion, peeled and coarsely chopped
2 tablespoons mayonnaise
Dash Worchestershire sauce
Salt and white pepper to taste

In the bowl of a food processor or mixer add all of the above ingredients. Blend until almost smooth, about 1 minute in a food processor and 2 to 3 minutes using a mixer.

If you are going to serve the dip within a short period of time, add half of the reserved juice to the clam mixture and blend until well mixed. Add all of the reserved clam juice to the clam mixture if you are making the dip a day ahead of when you plan on serving it. It seems to thicken on standing.

Serve with fresh potato chips.

Variation: Do not add the reserved juices. Spread the mixture on lightly toasted bread or English muffins. Pop them under the broiler for 1 minute or place in the microwave on high for 30 seconds until the topping starts to bubble and turn brown. Cut into bite-sized pieces and serve immediately.

MUSSELS WITH GARLIC BUTTER (Serves 8)

Prepare this appetizer in the morning and keep it in the refrigerator until you wish to serve it. This is a good recipe to use to introduce mussels to "first-time" mussel eaters.

24 medium-sized mussels or about 2 pounds, scrubbed
4 tablespoons butter, softened
1 clove garlic, minced
1/4 cup grated Parmesan cheese

Preheat the oven to broil.
Scrub the mussels and remove as much of the beard as possible with a pair of scissors. Place the mussels in a pot and barely cover with water. Place a lid on the pot and bring the water to a boil. .When the mussels pop open, place them in a colander and let them cool.
Remove any beard that might be remaining on the mussel by holding the mussel in one hand and giving a gentle tug on the beard with the other. Break each mussel shell in half. Place half of the mussel shell and its mussel in a single layer on a cookie sheet.
In a bowl mix the butter and garlic together. Place 1/2 teaspoon of the garlic butter mixture on top of each mussel followed by a good sprinkling of Parmesan cheese.
Place the cookie sheet under the broiler and broil for 1 minute or until the butter starts to bubble and the cheese is lightly browned. Serve immediately.

Microwave directions: Place the mussels in a shallow glass baking dish in a single layer. Microwave them on high for 30 seconds or until they pop open. Follow the above directions to prepare the individual mussels. Serve the mussels after you have heated them in the microwave for 30 seconds. Photo page 67.

CRAB PÂTE (Serves 6)

This delicious appetizer should be made a day ahead of when you plan to serve it for its flavor to be at its best.

1/2 pound picked crab
2 green onions
1 tablespoon soft butter
2 sprigs fresh parsley (reserve one for garnish)
1 tablespoon fresh lemon juice
1/2 cup mayonnaise
Salt and pepper to taste

Place all ingredients in the bowl of a food processor or blender and process until well blended, about 45 seconds. Pour the pâte into a small crock and chill for a minimum of two hours or overnight if possible. Garnish with a sprig of fresh parsley. Serve with thin rounds of dark bread or salted wholewheat crackers.

SHRIMP BUTTER (Serves 6)

Substitute crab, smoked salmon, smoked mussels or any leftover grilled fish such as a grilled salmon or steelhead, in place of the shrimp in this recipe.

1/2 pound butter
1/4 pound fresh bay shrimp
Salt and pepper to taste

Place all the ingredients in the bowl of a food processor or blender and process until well blended, about 45 seconds. (If you are using a blender melt the butter and let it cool slightly before blending.) Place the mixture in a small crock and chill for a minimum of two hours or overnight if possible. Serve with small slices of French bread or salted crackers. Photo page 69.

CRAYFISH COOKED WITH FRESH DILL (Serves 4)

One of the most exciting ways I have seen crayfish prepared for a large crowd was done by an acquaintance of mine. He cooked them, then transferred the lobster-red crayfish and their cooking juices to a large glass crock flavored by several heads of fresh dill. The guests, supplied with lots of fresh napkins and an abundance of cool beer, simply helped themselves to the delicate slivers of meat found in the tails and claws of these tiny creatures.

5 pounds live crayfish*
1 bottle dry white wine
2 sliced lemons (reserve 6 slices)
3 tablespoons rock salt
4 chopped shallots
1 head fresh dill (found in produce departments during the summer months)
Water to cover

Place all ingredients except the crayfish in a large kettle and bring to a boil. Add the crayfish and boil for 5 minutes or until the crayfish have turned a bright red color. Turn the heat off and let the pot sit for 5 more minutes. Remove the crayfish from the stock and let them both cool separately.

When they are both cool, place as many of the crayfish and as much of the fish stock as possible in a glass crock along with the dill and reserved lemon slices. Photo page 66.

*If you can only find crayfish already cooked, follow the above recipe but do not cook the crayfish. Bring the liquid to a boil and turn the heat off. When it has stopped boiling add the crayfish and let them cool in the liquid. Place the cooled crayfish and the stock in a glass crock along with the dill and reserved lemon slices.

ARTICHOKE HEARTS STUFFED WITH SMOKED SALMON
(Serves 4)

Artichoke hearts, or crowns, as they are sometimes called, can be purchased in several different forms: frozen, marinated, canned or fresh.

12 small artichoke hearts
3 ounces smoked salmon, coarsely chopped (reserve 12 small slivers of smoked salmon for garnish)
3 tablespoons mayonnaise
2 chopped green onions
3 sprigs chopped parsley

Preheat the oven to 400 degrees.
Place the artichoke hearts in a glass baking dish.
Combine the mayonnaise, green onions and parsley together in a small bowl or make the herb mayonnaise recipe on page 131.
Mix the salmon with the herb mayonnaise and place 1 teaspoon of the mixture inside each artichoke heart.
Bake the stuffed artichoke hearts for 8 - 10 minutes or until they are hot and bubbly. Garnish with the reserved slivers of smoked salmon and serve immediately. Photo page 68.
Microwave directions: Place the stuffed artichoke hearts in the microwave and heat on high for 30 - 45 seconds.

Variation: Follow the above recipe and serve chilled.

CRAB COCKTAIL WITH AVOCADO DRESSING (Serves 4)

The soft lime-green color of this dressing is a welcome change both visually and tastewise from the standard catsup-like cocktail sauce.

1 avocado
1 clove garlic, peeled
3/4 teaspoon fresh lemon juice
1 tablespoon mayonnaise
1 hard-boiled egg, cut into quarters
Salt and white pepper to taste
1 pound picked crab
4 lemon wedges

In the bowl of a food processor or blender place the avocado, garlic, lemon juice, mayonnaise and hard-boiled egg (cut the egg into small pieces if you are using a blender). Purée for 1 - 2 minutes or until the mixture is smooth. Season with salt and pepper.
Place 1/4 pound of crab in 4 small glass bowls. Scoop a large dollop of the dressing on top of the crab, dividing it equally between the 4 bowls.
Garnish each bowl with a lemon wedge and serve immediately. Photo page 67.

Variation: Substitute 1 pound of bay shrimp for the crab.

Appetizers

BROILED SCALLOPS WRAPPED IN PANCETTA (Serves 4)

Pancetta is often called "Italian bacon." It is cured pork made from the pork belly similar to American bacon but it is rolled during the curing process. It can be purchased in good delicatessens and its fine flavor is worth an extra shopping trip to find it. Substitute thinly sliced bacon if you cannot find it

8 ounces sea scallops
1/4 pound pancetta, thinly sliced

Cut the thinly sliced pancetta into 3-inch pieces. Lay a scallop on the edge of one piece of pancetta and roll it up, tucking in the sides as you go. Hold the pancetta in place with a toothpick. Repeat with each scallop.

Place the scallops wrapped in the pancetta on a broiling pan. Broil them for 3 - 4 minutes or until the pancetta is browned. Serve immediately.

Microwave instructions: Microwave the scallops wrapped in the pancetta on high for 2 - 3 minutes or until the scallop loses its translucency and the pancetta is lightly browned. Photo page 69

CREAM CHEESE AND CAVIAR (Serves 6 - 8)

Only roe from sturgeon can legally be called caviar. Specialty food stores that carry it usually keep the quality caviar under "lock and key." Substitute lumpfish roe in place of caviar if you want to keep expenses down; if you insist on having caviar you might consider selling one of your children to raise a little extra cash.

- 1 8-ounce package softened cream cheese, cut into eighths
- 1 teaspoon lemon juice
- 2 scallions, coarsely chopped
- 2 teaspoons caviar, or lumpfish roe
- 1 fresh lemon slice
- 2 sprigs fresh parsley

In the bowl of a food processor or mixer add the cream cheese, lemon juice and onions and blend until smooth, about 1 to 2 minutes. Remove the blade if you are using a food processor and gently stir in the caviar by hand. Place the mixture in a glass bowl. Garnish with a slice of fresh lemon and fresh parsley. Serve with unsalted crackers.

Variation: This can also be piped onto crackers or toast points by using a piping bag with a tip that has a large opening such as a 4 or 5B.

Appetizers

GRAVLAX

Gravlax is raw pickled salmon especially popular in the Scandinavian countries. This recipe calls for the addition of olive oil at the end of the pickling time which is not traditional but a favorite at our house.

1-1/2 pound salmon fillets or steelhead fillets, skin on
3 tablespoons salt
3 tablespoons sugar
1 teaspoon fresh dill, minced, or 1/2 teaspoon dried
1/2 cup mild olive oil

Rub the salt and sugar into the salmon meat. Cut the fillets in half and place one half, skin side down, on a large sheet of foil and sprinkle with the minced dill. Place the other half, skin side up, on top of the first half. Wrap the salmon tightly in the foil and place it in a shallow bowl. Let the fish cure for 8 hours.

Pour off the liquid that has accumulated in the bottom of the bowl. Place both pieces of fish skin side down in the bowl. Pour the olive oil over the salmon and let sit for 8 more hours.

SHRIMP AND GREEN ONIONS IN RED PEPPER BOATS
(Serves 4)

These colorful appetizers are easy to prepare and will keep up to 8 hours in the refrigerator once they are assembled.

- 2 red bellpeppers, seeded and cut in half lengthwise
- 1 cup bay shrimp (reserve 16 good-sized shrimp for garnish)
- 4 green onions, chopped
- 1 tablespoon mayonnaise
- Salt and pepper to taste

Mix the shrimp, green onions and mayonnaise together. Season with salt and pepper.

Cut each half of red bellpepper into 4 bite-sized pieces. Place the pieces of bell pepper skin side down on an attractive serving dish. Add a teaspoon of the shrimp mixture to each piece of pepper and garnish with a reserved shrimp.

Serve immediately or cover with plastic wrap and keep in the refrigerator for up to 8 hours.

Variation: Follow the recipe above and add a 1-by-1-inch piece of jack cheese, cut 1/4 inch thick, on top of each shrimp boat. Microwave them on high for 30 - 40 seconds or until the cheese melts. Do not overcook these appetizers or the red pepper will become soggy. Photo page 68.

Appetizers

SMOKED OYSTER SPREAD (Serves 6 - 8)

How many times have you opened a can of smoked oysters and had them disappear before you could even find the toothpicks? This recipe stretches one can of oysters about as far as it can go. It can be made several days before you need it.

    1 8-ounce package cream cheese
    1 3-3/4-ounce can smoked oysters and their juice
    1-1/2 teaspoon fresh dill or 1/2 teaspoon dried dill
    2 sprigs fresh parsley
    1/4 teaspoon salt
    1 scallion

Place all of the ingredients in the bowl of a food processor or blender and blend until smooth. Put the spread in a small crock and chill for a minimum of two hours or overnight if possible. Serve on your favorite cracker.

MOLDED SHRIMP APPETIZER (Serves 6 - 8)

This recipe was given to me by a friend when my husband was a graduate student. I do not know its origin so I cannot give proper credit to the originator. Whoever you are, "thank you." It has been a favorite appetizer and one that I have used over and over again. It can be made up to two days ahead of time.

1-1/2 teaspoons gelatin
1/2 cup cold water
3/4 cup dry white wine
1/2 pound fresh bay shrimp
1 tablespoon minced onion
1 teaspoon lemon juice
1/2 teaspoon dry mustard
1 cup mayonnaise

Soften the gelatin in cold water. Heat the wine and stir into the gelatin. Place half of the shrimp, the lemon juice, dry mustard and mayonnaise in the bowl of a food processor or blender and blend until smooth. Stir in the wine mixture and the reserved whole shrimp. Pour into a 2 cup mold and chill until set, about 3 hours. Unmold and serve as a spread with pumpernickel or rye cocktail rounds.

Variation: Substitute 1/2 pound smoked salmon or 1/2 pound picked crab for the shrimp. Photo page 70.

Salads

FRESH MUSHROOM AND SPINACH SALAD WITH CRAB LEGS (Serves 4)

Make this salad in the late springtime when tender young spinach is available in the markets.

1/2 cup mild olive oil
2 teaspoons lemon juice
1/2 teaspoon Grey Poupon mustard
1 clove garlic, minced
1/2 teaspoon tarragon, crushed
1/2 teaspoon salt
1/2 pound fresh mushrooms, cleaned and sliced vertically
1/2 pound crab legs
1 large head Boston (butter) lettuce, rinsed

Mix the olive oil, lemon juice, mustard, garlic, tarragon and salt together and pour over the mushrooms. Toss the mushrooms well to evenly distribute the dressing. Let the mushrooms sit at room temperature for 1 hour. Carefully fold in the crab legs and let the mixture marinate for 1 more hour.

Tear the lettuce into bite-sized pieces and place them in a large clear glass salad bowl. With a slotted spoon place the mushroom-crab mixture on top of the lettuce. Add enough of the dressing to the salad to coat each piece of lettuce and serve immediately. Photo page 71.

CURRIED CRAB ON BEEFSTEAK TOMATO SLICES
(Serves 4)

Serve this salad in the summertime when large, vine-ripened tomatoes are available.

1/2 pound fresh crab meat
1/2 cup mayonnaise
3 scallions, chopped
2 teaspoons mango chutney
1-1/2 teaspoon curry powder
Salt and white pepper to taste
8 slices of beefsteak tomato, about 1/2 inch thick
8 crisp lettuce leaves
16 black olives
8 midget sweet pickles

Place the crab meat, mayonnaise, scallions, chutney and curry powder in a bowl. Thoroughly mix the ingredients and season with salt and pepper.

Line four salad plates with the lettuce leaves. Place two tomato slices on each plate. Cover the slices with several heaping tablespoons of the crab mixture. Garnish each plate with three or four olives and several midget sweet pickles. Photo page 71.

DANISH POTATO SALAD WITH SMOKED CHINOOK SALMON (Serves 4)

Smoked chinook salmon is especially good served with potatoes and sour cream.

> 1 pound small new potatoes, cooked until barely tender and drained (unpeeled)
> 1/4 cup safflower oil
> 1 teaspoon wine vinegar
> 3 green onions, chopped
> 1/2 cup sour cream
> 6 ounces smoked chinook salmon, broken up into bite-sized pieces
> 1/4 cup chopped parsley
> 1/2 teaspoon capers (optional)
> Salt and white pepper to taste

While the potatoes are still warm cut them up into bite-sized pieces and place them in a bowl. Mix the oil and vinegar together and pour the dressing over the potatoes. Carefully toss the potatoes with a fork to distribute the dressing. Add the rest of the ingredients and toss again. Season with salt and pepper and chill for several hours before serving.

SIMPLE TUNA SALAD (Serves 4)

Not only is this salad delicious, it is also one of those recipes for which you usually have all of the ingredients on hand. Serve it on a hot summer evening with assorted crackers and sweetcream butter.

1 head green leaf lettuce, washed
1 6-1/2-ounce can tuna, drained
2 hard boiled eggs, peeled and coarsely chopped
2 green onions, chopped
10 cherry tomatoes
1/3 cup mayonnaise
1-1/2 tablespoons fresh lemon juice
Salt and pepper to taste

Tear the lettuce into bite-sized pieces and place them in a salad bowl. Add the tuna, eggs, green onions and cherry tomatoes to the lettuce.

In a bowl mix the mayonnaise and lemon juice together and pour the dressing over the salad ingredients, tossing well. Season with salt and pepper to taste.

Variation: Substitute left-over bite-sized pieces of grilled salmon or steelhead in place of the tuna.

SALADE NICOISE (Serves 4)

This is my own version of a salad that originated in the south of France. If you have a food processor or blender, the mayonnaise is simple to prepare and adds a flavorful touch to the salad.

2 pounds new potatoes, cooked, peeled and cubed
3 tablespoons safflower oil
2 teaspoons red wine vinegar
1 6-1/2-ounce can tuna, drained
8 ounces fresh green beans, cooked until barely tender, drained
4 hard-boiled eggs, cut into quarters
1/2 cup homemade mayonnaise (see page 130)
Salt and pepper to taste
8 Nicoise olives, Greek olives or black pitted olives
2 tomatoes, cut into wedges
4 anchovy fillets, optional
1 small head lettuce, washed

Place the potatoes in a large salad bowl. Mix the oil and vinegar together and pour if over the potatoes. Toss the potatoes in the dressing. Cut the green beans into 1 inch lengths and add them to the salad followed by the tuna. Break the tuna up into smaller pieces with a fork. Add the mayonnaise to the salad bowl and carefully toss the potatoes, beans, tuna and capers together.
Season with salt and pepper to taste.
Serve the salad on salad plates that have been lined with lettuce leaves. Garnish the top of the salad with the hard-boiled eggs, olives, tomato wedges and anchovy fillets.
Photo page 73.

MINCED SHRIMP, CELERY AND ONION IN A TANGY VINAIGRETTE (Serves 4)

This refreshing salad has been served every Thanksgiving and Christmas at my parents' house and at my grandmother's for as long as I can remember. It can be made up to 2 days ahead of time.

1 pound bay shrimp, coarsely chopped
2 large stalks celery, coarsely chopped
1 small yellow onion, coarsely chopped
1/3 cup safflower oil
1 - 2 teaspoons red wine vinegar
8 lettuce leaves, washed

Place the shrimp, celery and onion in a bowl. In a separate bowl beat the safflower oil and vinegar together until they are well mixed. Pour the vinaigrette over the salad ingredients and toss. Season with salt and freshly ground pepper. Let the salad marinate for two hours or overnight if possible before serving.

When you are ready to serve the salad, line four salad plates with the lettuce leaves. Place equal quantities of the salad on each plate and serve immediately. Photo page 72.

Variation I: In place of the oil and vinegar add 1/2 cup of mayonnaise. Mix all of the ingredients together. Remove the stem end of a beefsteak tomato. Make two slices in the tomato about an inch deep cutting it into quarters but not cutting it all the way through the bottom of the tomato. Place 1/2 cup of the salad mixture in the center of each tomato. Serve one tomato per person on a bed of lettuce garnished with slices of hard-boiled egg, black olives and midget sweet pickles.

Variation II: In place of the oil and vinegar add 1/2 cup of mayonnaise. Mix all of the ingredients together. Cut a ripe avocado in half and remove the pit. Place 1/2 cup of the salad mixture in the center of each avocado. Serve one avocado half per person on a bed of lettuce garnished with slices of hard boiled egg, black olives and midget sweet pickles.

TOSSED GREEN SALAD WITH COCKTAIL SHRIMP
(Serves 4)

The combination of the mild tasting shrimp and hard-boiled egg with this tangy salad dressing is a definite palate pleaser.

- 1 head leafy green lettuce, rinsed and torn into bite-sized pieces
- 8 ounces of bay shrimp
- 1 hard-boiled egg, chopped
- 2 green onions, chopped
- 1 tomato, cut into wedges
- 1/4 cup safflower oil
- 2 tablespoons red wine vinegar
- Salt and freshly ground pepper to taste

Place the lettuce, shrimp, egg, onions and tomatoes in a salad bowl.

Mix the oil and vinegar together and pour the dressing over the salad ingredients. Toss the salad and season it with salt and pepper.

SHRIMP COLESLAW (Serves 4)

This is my mother-in-law's recipe and a favorite of mine. Use fresh little bay shrimp and make it a day ahead for the best results.

- **1 head smooth green cabbage, cored and shredded**
- **1 large white onion, grated**
- **1 pound fresh bay shrimp**
- **1/2 cup mayonnaise**
- **Salt and pepper to taste**
- **2 sprigs fresh parsley**
- **1 lemon slice**

Mix the cabbage, onion and shrimp together with the mayonnaise. Season with salt and pepper and garnish with several sprigs of fresh parsley and a lemon slice.

PASTA SALAD WITH PESTO AND SMOKED SALMON (Serves 6)

The longer you keep this salad the better it gets. Put it in a covered container in the refrigerator and it will keep up to a week.

- **1 pound spinach fettucine, cooked, drained and still warm**
- **1/4 cup pesto (see page 113)**
- **1/2 cup freshly grated Parmesan cheese**
- **1/4 pound smoked chinook salmon, broken up into bite-sized pieces**

Place all of the ingredients in a large attractive serving bowl and toss them together until they are well mixed. Chill for several hours before serving.

Fresh smelt ready to be cooked, page 14

Antipasto Platter with Herb Mayonnaise and Garlicky Shrimp, pages 42, 109

Clams Stuffed with Dungeness Crab and Cream Cheese, page 44

Crayfish Cooked with Fresh Dill, page 48

Crab Cocktail with Avocado Dressing, page 50

Mussels with Garlic Butter, page 46

Artichoke Hearts Stuffed with Smoked Salmon, page 49

Shrimp and Green Onion in Red Pepper Boats, page 54

Shrimp Butter, page 47

Broiled Scallops Wrapped in Pancetta, page 51

Molded Shrimp Appetizer, page 56

Lox, Capers and Marinated Onions on Butter Lettuce, page 81

Curried Crab on Beefsteak Tomato Slices, page 58

Fresh Mushroom and Spinach Salad with Crab Legs, page 57

Marinated Cocktail Artichoke Salad with Shrimp, page 83

Minced Shrimp, Celery and Onion in a Tangy Vinaigrette, page 62

Salad Nicoise, page 61

Dungeness Crab and Clam Cioppino, page 84

Mussel Bisque with Saffron, page 88

Garlicky Jumbo Shrimp, page 109

Broiled Salmon Steaks with Lime Butter and Fresh Herbs, page 115

Fettucine Ruelle, page 116

Poached Steelhead with Pancetta and Rosemary, page 119

Steamer Clams Cooked with Garlic and Rosemary, page 100

Catfish Meunière, page 94

Sturgeon Provençale, page 120

Mint-Stuffed Rainbow Trout, page 125

Halibut and Prosciutto with Shish Kebab, page 101

Teriyaki Lingcod with Fresh Ginger, page 102

Fresh Crab with Purée of Leek Au Gratin, page 95

Oysters Florentine, page 103

Raw Oysters with Cocktail Sauce, page 133

LOX, CAPERS, AND MARINATED ONIONS ON BUTTER LETTUCE (Serves 4)

Although this is a rather simple salad it makes a stunning first course. It should be served with thick slices of crusty French bread and a glass of dry white wine.

1 large red onion, peeled and thinly sliced
1/2 cup mild olive oil
1 tablespoon wine vinegar
1/2 teaspoon Grey Poupon mustard
1/2 pound thinly sliced lox
2 teaspoons capers
1 head butter lettuce, washed
4 lemon wedges

Place the onion slices in a shallow bowl.

Whisk together the olive oil, vinegar and mustard until it is well mixed and pour the dressing over the onions. Let the onions marinate up to 8 hours.

Divide the butter lettuce evenly between 4 salad plates. Arrange 2 - 3 slices of lox on each plate and sprinkle the slices with 1/2 teaspoon of the capers. Place 1/2 cup of the marinated onions next to the lox and drizzle some of the marinade from the onions over all.

Place a lemon wedge on each plate. Photo page 70.

RICE SALAD WITH BAY SHRIMP AND FRESH HERBS
(Serves 6)

Rice salads are a refreshing change from the ubiquitous potato salad. Make this salad a day before you plan on serving it so that all its many flavors have time to meld together.

> 3 cups cooked long grain white rice, warm or at room temperature
> 2 tablespoons wine vinegar or lemon juice
> 1/2 cup olive oil
> 1/2 cup mayonnaise
> 1/2 cup coarsely chopped red bell pepper
> 1/2 cup sliced green onions
> 1 tablespoon minced parsley
> 1 tablespoon minced dill
> 1/2 pound fresh bay shrimp
> Salt and pepper to taste

Mix the vinegar and olive oil and pour it over the rice. After thoroughly tossing the rice and dressing together add the rest of the ingredients and toss the salad again. Season with salt and pepper. This is an especially good summer salad.

MARINATED COCKTAIL ARTICHOKE SALAD WITH SHRIMP   (Serves 4)

Cocktail artichokes can often be found in specialty food shops in the produce section. They are about 2 inches long and so tender they can be eaten whole without removing the choke. If you cannot find them substitute quarters of cooked artichokes that have had the choke removed or a jar of marinated artichoke hearts.

1/3 cup olive oil
2 cloves garlic, minced
1/2 pound medium sized shrimp, cooked and peeled (see page 35)
1 red bell pepper, cut into 2 in. x 1/4 in. strips
4 lemon slices
3 sprigs minced parsley
1/2 cup black or green stuffed olives or a mixture of both
8 cherry tomatoes
4 pepperoncini
8 cocktail artichokes, cooked
8 lettuce leaves
Salt and pepper to taste

While the artichokes are still warm, place them in a shallow bowl along with the rest of the ingredients except the lettuce leaves. Let the salad marinate for 2 hours or overnight.

Line 4 salad plates with the lettuce leaves and equally divide the salad among them.

Variation: This is an attractive salad to take along on picnics in a 1 quart old-fashioned hinged canning jar. Serve it from the jar with a slotted spoon or a fondue fork and let everyone help themselves. Photo page 72.

Soups

DUNGENESS CRAB AND CLAM CIOPPINO (Serves 8)

Crab cioppino is made from a deep red tomato-based sauce which is used to cook the shellfish and for this reason it is very different from the light saffron flavored stock of bouillabaisse. Whenever there is leftover cioppino sauce at our house it is served the following evening over fresh pasta.

3 tablespoons olive oil
2 large onions, chopped
7 cloves garlic, minced
4 15-ounce cans tomato sauce
2 - 3 teaspoons Italian herb seasoning
3 cups dry white wine, such as a Chardonnay
4 cooked crabs, cleaned, jointed and cracked
3 pounds butterclams (in shells)
Salt and pepper to taste
3 sprigs fresh parsley, chopped

Sauté the onions in olive oil until the onions start to turn a golden brown, about 8 minutes. Add the garlic, tomato sauce, water, tomato paste, seasonings and wine. Simmer gently for 2 - 3 hours. Twenty minutes before you wish to eat add the crab and continue to simmer gently. Five minutes before the cooking time is up add the clams.

When the clams have popped open the cioppino is ready to be served. Season the soup with salt and pepper. Serve in individual warmed soup bowls with a sprinkle of freshly chopped parsley. Photo page 73.

CREAM OF CRAB BISQUE WITH MUSHROOMS AND SHERRY (Serves 4)

Before you start this recipe get out your good crystal and pour yourself a glass of sherry. Hopefully it will be after five o'clock or at least after five o'clock somewhere in the world.

3 tablespoons butter
1 small onion, coarsely chopped
12 ounces of mushrooms, cleaned and sliced
3 tablespoons flour
1/2 pound fresh crab meat, out of the shell
3 cups half and half
1/3 cup dry sherry
Salt and pepper to taste

Heat the butter in a large pot. Place the onions in the pot and cook until they turn transparent, about 5 minutes. Put the mushrooms in with the onions and cook for 5 more minutes, or until the mushrooms start to soften. Sprinkle the flour over the mushrooms and onions and cook over moderate heat for 3 minutes. Stir the mushrooms and flour with a wooden spoon to keep them from sticking.

Pour in the half and half and sherry and stir the soup over medium heat until it thickens. Season with salt and pepper to taste. Serve immediately in warmed soup bowls.

BOUILLABAISSE (Serves 6 - 8)

The name bouillabaisse, pronounced "boo-ya-bess," was derived from an old French word, *bouiabaisso* which means "boil stop." The secret of this recipe is to boil the soup so that the oil and water will mix and to stop the boiling when the fish is perfectly cooked. It is rumored that bouillabaisse was created by Venus as a sleeping potion for her husband, Vulcan, while she pursued other activities. I have not verified this recipe as a sleeping potion so take your own chances.

- 3/4 cup onions, coarsely chopped
- 1/3 cup olive oil
- 5 cloves garlic, crushed
- 2 cups tomatoes, coarsely chopped
- 2 pinches saffron
- 3 sprigs fresh parsley, finely chopped
- 1/2 teaspoon dried basil or 1-1/2 teaspoon fresh
- 2-1/2 quarts fish stock (see page 128)
- 4 pounds fish and shellfish*, cut into bite-sized pieces (choose from the list below).

Sauté the onion in the olive oil until it starts to turn a golden brown, about 5 - 8 minutes. Add the garlic, tomatoes, saffron, parsley, basil and fish stock and boil for 20 more minutes.

Ten minutes before serving add the crab and firm-textured fish such as halibut. Cook for 5 minutes. Add the remaining ingredients and boil for 5 minutes more. Season with salt and pepper and serve in warmed soup bowls.

*Winter and Early Spring

- 2 pounds king crab or 2 pounds Dungeness crab
- 1/2 pound red snapper
- 1/2 pound halibut
- 1 pound scallops
- 2 pounds steamer clams
- 1 pound mussels
- 1 lobster

Late Spring, Summer, Fall

2 pounds Dungeness crab
1 pound sablefish (black cod)
1/2 pound halibut
1/2 pound chinook salmon
1/2 pound sturgeon
1/2 pound prawns
1 pound mussels
8 crayfish

SMOKED MUSSEL BISQUE (Serves 2)

Smoked mussels are a new arrival in American fish markets. They are delicious eaten plain with an herb mayonnaise or in a soup such as in this recipe.

1/2 cup chopped onion
2 tablespoons butter
1/2 pound smoked mussels
1/2 cup dry white wine
1/2 teaspoon whole thyme, crushed
2 sprigs parsley, chopped
1 cup cream
Salt and pepper to taste

Sauté the onions in the butter for 5 - 8 minutes or until they start to turn golden brown. Add the remaining ingredients, except the cream, and bring to a boil. Add the cream and heat until it just starts to boil. Season with salt and pepper. Serve immediately in warmed soup bowls.

MUSSEL BISQUE WITH SAFFRON (Serves 2)

The mussels found in the Pacific Northwest are a beautiful brilliant orange color when they are cooked, a perfect contrast to their black shells. Add a sprinkling of chopped parsley to this tasty soup to make a stunning presentation at the table.

1 pound fresh mussels, small to medium-sized
1/2 cup dry white wine
1/2 cup water
1/2 cup chopped onion
7 - 8 peppercorns
1/2 bay leaf
1/2 teaspoon whole thyme, crushed
1 cup cream
1 large pinch saffron
Salt and white pepper to taste
2 sprigs parsley, chopped

Wash the mussels thoroughly in cold water, taking off as much of the beard as possible. Place the wine, water, onions, peppercorns, bay leaf and thyme in a pot and bring to a boil. Add the mussels and cook them until they open, about 5 - 8 minutes.

Strain the broth through cheesecloth and place it along with the cream and saffron in a saucepan and set aside.

Remove each mussel from its shell and discard all of the beard remnants. Add the mussels to the broth mixture and gently heat. Season with salt and pepper. Serve piping hot in warmed soup bowls with a sprinkling of freshly chopped parsley. Photo page 74.

CREAMY CLAM CHOWDER (Serves 4)

Just the thought of a rich, creamy clam chowder makes me hungry. I prefer to use either the geoduck or the Martha Washington clam although almost any clam will work. Many fish markets carry freshly chopped clams. If you prefer to chop your own run them through an old-fashioned meat grinder using the 3/16-inch plate or chop them in the food processor using the steel blade.

1/4 pound bacon, cut into bite-sized pieces
1 large onion, chopped
1/4 cup flour
1-1/2 pounds clams, coarsely chopped
1 pound red new potatoes, cooked and cubed (not peeled)
1 quart half and half
Salt and pepper to taste
2 sprigs fresh parsley, chopped

Sauté the bacon and onion together until the onions start to brown and the bacon is cooked, about 8 minutes. Pour off any fat that has accumulated in the bottom of the pan. Add the clams to the bacon and onions and sprinkle with the flour. Cook this mixture over medium heat, stirring constantly, for 3 minutes.

Add the half and half and stir the mixture over medium-high heat until the soup thickens. Add the potatoes and season with salt and pepper to taste. Serve garnished with chopped parsley.

OYSTER STEW (Serves 3 - 4)

This stew should be in the *Two Minute Gourmet Cookbook* because that is about how long it takes to make it.

1 pint fresh medium-sized oysters with liquor, cut into eighths
1/4 cup water
1/4 cup dry vermouth
2 cups half and half
2 tablespoons chopped parsley
Salt and pepper to taste
4 teaspoons butter

Place the oyster liquor, oysters, water and vermouth in a heavy skillet and simmer until the edges of the oysters curl, about 1 minute. Add the half and half and gently heat until hot. Season with salt and pepper.

Ladle into warmed soup bowls and dot each with a teaspoon of butter. Sprinkle with fresh parsley and serve immediately.

CREAM OF CHANTERELLE SOUP WITH SMOKED SALMON (Serves 3 - 4)

Chanterelle mushrooms, or girolles as the French call them, are indigenous to many regions in the United States. They are trumpet shaped and a beautiful apricot color which makes them easy to spot in the deep green moss of the forest floor.

1-1/2 pounds chanterelles, sliced
3 tablespoons butter
1 cup chicken broth
1 cup cream
1/4 pound smoked salmon, coarsely chopped
Salt and pepper to taste

Sauté the chanterelles in butter and cook until they become soft and white, about 10 minutes. Place the chanterelles and the cooking juices in a food processor or blender and purée until the mixture becomes homogenous. Push this mixture through a sieve to eliminate any large pieces of mushroom that still remain.

Place the puréed mushrooms back in a pan and stir in the cream, smoked salmon and chicken broth. Season with salt and pepper if necessary. Serve immediately in warmed soup bowls.

Entrées

ABALONE BAKED IN ITS SHELL   (Serves 4)

This recipe was given to Gary Evans, a "blood brother" of my husband's from high school, by an old-timer in northern California. If you are fortunate enough to have gathered some abalone, this is a delightful way to prepare them. Build a large fire on the open beach when the sun is just starting to set and pour yourself a glass of vintage dry white wine to warm you while the abalone cooks.

1 abalone, cleaned, with the foot removed
2 abalone shells
1/2 teaspoon fresh dill or 1/4 teaspoon dried
2 tablespoons butter
Salt and pepper to taste

Pound the whole abalone with a mallet or an empty beer bottle if you do not happen to have a mallet lying around. Slice the abalone into 4 to 5 steaks, about 1/4 inch thick. Butter each steak and sprinkle with salt, pepper and a small amount of dill.

Put the abalone back together again and wrap it in tinfoil. Place the abalone inside one abalone shell and press a second shell on top of the foil. The foil will keep the shells intact.

Place the abalone in the hot coals and cook for 20 minutes or until the meat is done.

Entrées

CATFISH PARMESAN WITH A COULIS OF TOMATO
(Serves 2)

A coulis is a purée and in this recipe it is made from fresh tomatoes, garlic and parsley.

2 medium tomatoes, quartered
3 sprigs parsely
1 clove garlic
Salt
1 teaspoon milk
1 egg
1/2 cup grated Parmesan cheese
1 pound catfish, cut into fillets, cleaned and skinned
4 lemon slices

Preheat the oven to broil. Set the oven rack 4 inches from the broiler.

Place the tomatoes, 2 sprigs of parsley, garlic and a dash of salt in the bowl of a food processor or blender and process until puréed, about 40 seconds. Pour the purée into a non-aluminum pan and cook over high heat until most of the liquid has evaporated and the mixture has thickened. Cover and set aside.

Beat the milk and eggs together until well blended. Dip the catfish fillets into this mixture and then roll them in the Parmesan cheese. Place the fillets on a broiler pan and broil 3 minutes on each side. They are done when the flesh can be pierced easily with a fork.

Place the fish on a warmed platter and pour the coulis of tomato over the fish. Garnish with lemon slices and fresh parsley.

Variation: Substitute any of the soles in place of the catfish.

CATFISH MEUNIÈRE (Serves 2)

Catfish are often thought of as trash fish but nothing could be farther from the truth. They are a delicious fish with flesh that is firm and moist. The common catfish, raised commercially in the South, is the nation's leading aquaculture fish.

1/4 cup butter
1 pound catfish, cleaned and skinned
1/3 cup flour
Salt and freshly ground pepper
Juice of 1/2 lemon
2 sprigs parsley, minced
1 teaspoon capers (optional)

Melt two tablespoons of butter in a large skillet.

Dust the fish with the flour and season with salt and pepper. Fry the catfish in the hot butter 3 - 4 minutes a side. When the fish is cooked, place it on a warmed platter.

Add the remaining butter, lemon juice, parsley and capers to the pan. Heat until the butter bubbles and browns slightly, scraping the bottom of the pan as it heats. Pour over the fish and serve immediately. Photo page 77.

Entrées

FRESH CRAB WITH PURÉE OF LEEK AU GRATIN (WITH CRAYFISH GARNISH) (Serves 4)

I make this simple crab dish in an attractive baking dish and serve it at the table from the dish. One crayfish used as a garnish makes a spectacular presentation.

1 bunch of fresh leeks, about 12 ounces
1/2 cup grated Gruyère cheese
1/2 cup grated cheddar cheese
3 eggs
1-1/2 cup half and half
1/2 teaspoon salt
1/4 teaspoon white pepper
1 pound fresh crab meat
1 crayfish, cooked

Preheat the oven to 375 degrees.

Split the leeks down the middle and wash in cold water. Trim 1 inch off the green end. Cut the remaining leek into 1 inch pieces and cook in a small amount of salted water until barely tender. Drain the cooked leeks and purée them in a food processor or blender.

Beat the eggs, half and half, and the salt and pepper together until well mixed.

Grease a 9-inch glass pie pan or au gratin dish and spread the purée of leek on the bottom. Sprinkle the fresh crab on top of the leeks. Place the grated cheeses on top of the crab. Carefully pour the egg mixture over all.

Bake until a knife inserted in the middle of the dish comes out clean, about 30 minutes. Remove from the oven and let it sit at room temperature for 5 minutes. Garnish with a freshly cooked crayfish and fresh parsley. Photo page 79.

HOT DUNGENESS CRAB WITH SPICY GINGER SAUCE
(Serves 4)

Many years ago we celebrated Chinese New Year dining in a Chinese restaurant in Portland's Chinatown. The most outstanding dish of the evening was a huge bowl of hot gingered crab. Here is my re-creation of this classic Chinese dish which can be served either hot or cold.

- 4 tablespoons safflower oil
- 2 Dungeness crabs, cleaned, cracked and jointed
- 1 tablespoon fresh ginger, grated
- 4 scallions, coarsely chopped
- 1/2 cup soy sauce
- 1/4 cup sesame oil
- 1 teaspoon sugar
- 3 cloves garlic, peeled and minced

Place the 4 tablespoons of safflower oil in a large deep skillet and add the crab, ginger and scallions. Cook over medium-high heat until the crab meat gets warm, about 10 minutes.

In a bowl stir the soy sauce, sesame oil and sugar together and pour the mixture over the crab. Toss the minced garlic over all and cook until the crab is hot, about 10 more minutes. (Remember that crab is already cooked and just needs to be heated before serving.) This dish can be easily reheated the following day on top of the stove or by placing it in the microwave and cooking on high for 1 minute.

Entrées

CRAB LEGS SAUTÉED IN MADEIRA AND BRANDY
(Serves 4)

Serve these savory morsels the night you invite the boss to dinner. If you are the boss serve them any night you want; who could be more important? And, if you are not the boss but you would like to be, serve them to impress clients and use your expense account.

    3 tablespoons butter
    2 teaspoons Grey Poupon mustard
    1-1/2 teaspoons lemon juice
    2 tablespoons Madeira
    2 tablespoons brandy
    3/4 pound fresh crab legs, shelled
    2 sprigs fresh parsley, chopped
    4 slices lemon

In a sauté pan heat the butter. Stir in the mustard, lemon juice, Madeira and brandy. Cook for 3 minutes stirring constantly.

Add the crab legs and toss with the sauce. Cook over high heat until the crab is hot, about 4 minutes. Serve them on warm plates with buttered rice or noodles. Garnish with fresh parsley and a lemon slice.

SAUTÉED CRAB MEAT PATTIES   (Serves 3)

Serve these delicious crab meat patties hot or cold with a large green salad, crusty French bread and a bottle of dry white wine.

1 pound fresh crab meat
2 eggs
1/2 cup Parmesan cheese, grated
1 clove garlic, minced
1 shallot, chopped, or 1 chopped green onion
1/4 cup minced fresh parsley
1/2 teaspoon salt or salt to taste
1/4 teaspoon white pepper

Mix all ingredients together and shape them into 3 patties. Sauté them in butter until lightly browned, about 5 minutes a side.

Entrées

QUICK-FRIED RAZOR CLAMS (Serves 4)

Fresh razor clams are a wonderful delicacy that need little added to them to improve their flavor. This recipe is the traditional method for cooking these bivalves. Realistically, they do not need to be cooked, but just warmed throughout.

4 tablespoons butter plus 2 teaspoons
1/4 cup safflower oil
1 cup flour
1 egg
1/4 cup milk
2 pound razor clams, ready for cooking
1-1/2 cups fresh cracker crumbs or corn meal
Juice from 1 lemon
2 sprigs fresh parsley
Salt and pepper to taste

In a large skillet heat 4 tablespoons of butter and the safflower oil. Place the milk and egg together in a shallow bowl and beat them together until they are well mixed. Put the flour and cracker crumbs on separate sheets of wax paper.

Dredge the clams, one by one, first in the flour, then in the milk-egg mixture and finally roll them in the cracker crumbs. When the butter and oil is very hot, quickly fry the clams 2 - 3 minutes a side or until the clams are well heated. Place them on a warmed platter and season with salt and pepper.

Place 2 teaspoons of butter and the lemon juice in the same skillet and turn the heat to medium high. Swirl the butter around with a wooden spoon, scraping loose the concentrated cooked bits on the bottom of the pan as you do so. After 1 - 2 minutes pour the sauce over the clams, garnish with fresh parsley and serve immediately.

STEAMER CLAMS COOKED WITH GARLIC AND ROSEMARY (Serves 4)

These versatile little clams disappear in a hurry at the dinner table. They can also be served as an appetizer with tall glasses of ice cold beer.

2 tablespoons olive oil
2 pounds steamer clams
1/3 cup dry white wine
3 cloves garlic, chopped
1/2 teaspoon rosemary, chopped

In a shallow skillet with a lid add the olive oil, clams and wine. Sprinkle the clams with the chopped garlic and rosemary. Place a lid on the pan and turn the heat to high. Bring the wine to a boil and cook until the clams pop open, about 3- 5 minutes.

Microwave directions: Place all of the ingredients in a rectangular glass baking dish. Cover with plastic wrap and microwave on high until the clams pop open, about 1 minute. Photo page 76.

Entrées

HALIBUT AND PROSCIUTTO SHISH KEBABS
(Serves 4)

Halibut is a type of flounder that has firm, dense meat. It needs plenty of salt and pepper and caution needs to be taken not to overcook it or it will be dry. Prosciutto, also called Italian ham, can be purchased at most delicatessens.

1 pound halibut steaks, skin removed
1/4 cup olive oil
1/4 cup safflower oil
1 clove garlic, minced
Salt and freshly ground pepper
1/4 pound prosciutto thinly sliced
1 red bell pepper, seeded and cut into 1 inch squares
1 red onion, peeled and cut into eighths
4 tablespoons butter, melted
2 teaspoons fresh lemon juice
4 skewers

Place the halibut steaks in a shallow bowl. Mix the two oils together and pour them over the fish. Sprinkle the garlic, salt and pepper over the steaks and let them marinate for 2 hours, turning the steaks over 2 or 3 times.

Remove the halibut from the marinade and cut the fish and the prosciutto into 1-inch squares.

Preheat the oven to broil.

Divide the halibut into 4 equal portions. Start with 1 of the skewers and add a piece of prosciutto followed by a piece of halibut, onion and red pepper. Follow this same procedure until the skewer is full. Repeat for the other 3 skewers and place them on a broiler pan.

Brush the shish kebabs with the oil marinade and broil for 5 minutes, turning the fish halfway through the cooking process until the fish is done.

Add the lemon juice to the melted butter. Liberally brush the cooked shish kebabs with the melted butter and serve immediately. Photo page 78.

TERIYAKI LINGCOD WITH FRESH GINGER (Serves 4)

Lingcod is a wonderful tasting fish that is moist with large, tender flakes. This recipe uses Hoisin sauce, a flavorful sauce made from soybeans, which can be found at most grocery stores with the Chinese hardgoods.

2 tablespoons butter
2 tablespoons Hoisin sauce
2 tablespoons soy sauce
2 cloves garlic, crushed
2 - 3 thin slices fresh ginger, not peeled
1-1/2 pounds lingcod
2 sprigs fresh parsley

Preheat the oven to broil.
Put all the ingredients except the fish in a saucepan and heat until the mixture boils.
Place the fish on a broiling pan and brush both sides of the fish with the soy sauce mixture. Broil the fish 4 minutes and turn them over. Brush them with the sauce and broil for 4 more minutes or until the fish is done. The flesh should flake easily with a fork. Place the fish on a warmed platter and brush the top side of the fish with the sauce once again. Garnish with fresh parsley and serve immediately. Photo page 79.

Entrées

OYSTERS FLORENTINE   (Serves 4)

This recipe works well in the microwave. It can also be served as an appetizer in which case you use smaller scallop shells.

1 10-ounce jar small oysters, drained
1/2 cup cooked spinach, drained and puréed
4 large scallop shells

Preheat the oven to 350 degrees.
Place two oysters in each scallop shell.
Make the Hollandaise sauce following the recipe below. Carefully fold the Hollandaise sauce into the puréed spinach. Equally divide the spinach sauce between the 4 scallop shells. Bake for 10 minutes. Serve immediately. Photo page 80.

Microwave directions: Microwave for 2 minutes on medium.

Hollandaise Sauce

2 egg yolks
1-1/2 teaspoons lemon juice
1 tablespoon hot water
1/8 teaspoon salt
Few grains cayenne pepper
8 tablespoons hot melted butter

Warm the container of a food processor or blender with warm water. Pour out the water and dry it out with a dish towel. Add the egg yolks, lemon juice, hot water, salt and cayenne pepper to the container and turn the machine on. With the machine still running, slowly add the hot melted butter while the sauce gradually thickens.

Variation: Substitute one pound of scallops for the oysters.

BAKED PERCH WITH SOUR CREAM AND CHILES
(Serves 4)

1-1/2 pounds perch
Salt and pepper
4 slices red onion
4 lemon slices
1/3 cup jalapeno chiles, seeded and chopped
1 cup sour cream
1/2 cup cilantro, chopped

Warm four dinner plates.
Preheat the oven to 375 degrees.
Arrange the fish in a buttered baking dish and sprinkle with salt and pepper. Break the onion slices up into rings and lay them on the fish. Place the lemon slices on top of the onion and set the dish, uncovered, in the oven. Bake for 10 minutes.
Mix the sour cream and chiles together.
Remove the dish from the oven and pour the sour cream-chile mixture over all. Bake for 8 more minutes or until the fish flakes easily and the sour cream is hot. Place on warmed dinner plates and garnish with chopped cilantro. Serve with a savory rice dish, such as Spanish rice.

Entrées

SAUTÉED SABLEFISH WITH SALSA   (Serves 4)

Cilantro is an herb that is also called "Chinese parsley." It can be purchased in Chinese grocery stores or in the produce section of large supermarkets.

2/3 cup flour
1 teaspoon ground cumin
1-1/2 - 2 tablespoons safflower oil
1-1/2 pounds sablefish
2 cups salsa, canned or fresh (recipe follows)
4 tablespoons sour cream
4 sprigs cilantro or parsley
Salt and pepper to taste

Warm 4 dinner plates.

Mix the flour and cumin together on a sheet of wax paper. Dust each piece of fish in the mixture.

Place the salsa in a small pan and gently heat.

Pour the safflower oil in a frying pan and heat until it is very hot.

Add the fish and sauté for 5 minutes or until the bottom side of the fish is golden brown. Turn the fish over and cook for 2 more minutes or until the fish flakes easily with a fork. Season with salt and pepper.

Place the cooked fish on the warmed plates. With a ladle, pour the salsa over the fish, dividing it equally among the 4 plates. Top with a tablespoon of sour cream and a sprig of cilantro.

SALSA

6 tomatillas, husks removed
1 cup water
2 large cloves garlic, minced
1/4 cup chopped onion
1/4 cup chopped cilantro
Salt to taste

Place the water in a small pot and bring to a boil. Add the tomatillas and cook for 10 minutes to soften. Remove them from the water and coarsely chop.* Place all of the ingredients together in a small bowl and mix well. Season with salt and pepper. Add a small amount of water if the mixture is too thick.

*If using a food processor, place the cooked tomatillas and the rest of the ingredients in the work bowl. Process for 30 - 45 seconds or until the mixture is coarsely chopped.

Entrées

SKATE WINGS WITH LEMON BUTTER AND CAPERS
(Serves 4)

Skate wings are one of the least expensive items in the fish market and one of the most flavorful. Do not let their unusual appearance deter you. Their basic structure includes long slender bones that run the length of the wings which are covered by a thick-looking layer of skin. Once they are cooked the tender white meat simply falls off the bone and the heat causes the skin to separate itself from the meat.

3-1/2 pounds skate wings, cut into 3-by-3-inch squares
1/2 cup butter
1/4 cup wine vinegar
3 sprigs parsley, minced
Juice of 1/2 lemon
1 tablespoon capers

Sauté the skate wings in a small amount of butter until done, about 8 - 10 minutes, depending on their thickness. They should flake easily when tested with a fork. Place them on a warmed platter.

Turn the heat to high and add the rest of the ingredients to the pan. Stir to mix all the ingredients together and when the butter has melted pour the sauce over the fish. Serve immediately.

SHRIMP POACHED IN WHITE WINE   (Serves 4)

This simple method for cooking shrimp is quick and easy for a pleasant summer dinner. Cook the shrimp in the morning, let them cool and place them in the refrigerator until you are ready to eat. Serve the shrimp in a large glass bowl and let everyone peel their own. As an accompaniment, make the lemon mayonnaise and use it as a dipping sauce for the shrimp.

1 pound medium-sized shrimp
1 cup dry white wine
2 cloves garlic, crushed
1 bay leaf
10 peppercorns
4 lemon slices

Place all the ingredients in a large pot and add enough water to cover the shrimp. Turn on the heat and bring them to a boil. Boil for 3 minutes only. Remove from the heat and let cool in the poaching liquid. Drain and serve with lemon mayonnaise.

Microwave directions: Place all of the above ingredients in a shallow glass bowl and add enough water to barely cover. Cover the bowl with plastic wrap and microwave on high for 45 seconds to 1 minute.

LEMON MAYONNAISE

1 whole egg
1 teaspoon fresh lemon juice
1/2 teaspoon grated lemon rind
3 tablespoons chopped chives
1/2 teaspoon salt
1-1/2 cups safflower oil
White pepper to taste

Place all the ingredients except the oil in the bowl of a food processor or blender. Blend for 20 seconds then, with the machine still running, slowly add the oil drop by drop.

Entrées

Continue adding the oil as the mayonnaise gradually thickens. Season with pepper to taste.

GARLICKY JUMBO SHRIMP (Serves 4)

The secret of this recipe is to *not brown the garlic* when you heat the butter. Garlic tends to burn easily and its flavor will be at its best when it is added at the end of the cooking process.

  2 tablespoons butter
  1 pound large shrimp, peeled
  2 large cloves garlic, minced
  3 sprigs parsley, minced
  4 lemon slices

Heat the butter in a sauté pan. Cut each shrimp lengthwise down the outside center 1/4 inch deep or just enough to cut the shrimp in half but to still have it joining at the front. This is called butterflying.

When the butter has melted and is very hot, add the shrimp and quickly sauté them. This should take about 2 minutes. Add the minced garlic and parsley and serve immediately on warmed plates with fresh lemon slices. Photo page 74.

WHOLEWHEAT CRÊPES STUFFED WITH FRESH SHRIMP AND SOUR CREAM (Serves 4)

Wholewheat pastry flour can be purchased at health food stores. It also makes a tasty pie crust for vegetarian pies.

Crêpes

    1 cup wholewheat pastry flour
    1-1/2 cups milk
    3 eggs
    2 tablespoons melted butter, cooled
    1/4 teaspoon salt

Filling

    1 pound fresh bay shrimp
    2 teaspoons fresh dill, minced, or 1/2 teaspoon dried dill
    1 cup sour cream
    2 cups grated Gruyère cheese
    Salt and white pepper to taste
    Sprig of fresh dill or parsley for garnish

Preheat the oven to 350 degrees.

Blend the crepê batter ingredients together in a food processor or blender until the batter becomes smooth, about 45 seconds. Make the crêpes in a well greased 6 inch crêpe pan. Place them in a single layer on waxed paper to cool.

Mix together the filling. Season with salt and pepper to taste.

Fill each crêpe with 2 tablespoons of the filling and roll the crêpe lengthwise. Place them seamside down in a greased 9-by-9-inch baking dish. Cover them with foil and bake for 30 minutes.

Serve with a dollop of sour cream on top of each crêpe and garnish with a piece of fresh dill or parsley.

Microwave directions: Microwave on high for 1 minute.

SHRIMP BAKED IN FILO   (Serves 4)

Filo is an extremely thin type of Greek pastry that is used for both savory and sweet dishes. It can be found in delicatessens or in the frozen food department at most grocery stores.

1 small onion, chopped
8 tablespoons unsalted butter, melted
10 fresh mushrooms, cleaned and sliced
1/2 red bell pepper, chopped
1/2 pound fresh bay shrimp
2 sprigs fresh dill, minced or 1/2 teaspoon dried
Salt and pepper to taste
8 sheets filo
3 ounces cream cheese, softened

Preheat the oven to 350 degrees.

Sauté the onions in 2 teaspoons of butter until they start to turn brown, about 8 minutes. Add the mushrooms and red pepper and cook for 3 - 4 minutes, or until the vegetables start to soften. Remove from heat and stir in shrimp and dill. Season with salt and pepper and let cool.

Brush 1 sheet of filo dough liberally with butter. Place another filo sheet directly on top of the first piece and brush it with butter. Repeat this process until all 8 sheets of filo are buttered and layered.

Distribute the shrimp evenly over the buttered filo leaving 3 inches uncovered on each short end and along one long side. (The uncovered filo permits the filo and its filling to be rolled.)

Dot with the cream cheese and fold both short ends in towards the middle and brush with butter. Fold the long side over the shrimp mixture and roll towards the long edge with the 3-inch margin. Place the roll on an unbuttered cookie sheet, seam side down, and brush the entire roll with butter. Bake at 350 degrees for 30 minutes or until the filo is lightly browned.

LEEK AND SHRIMP QUICHE WITH FRESH DILL
(Serves 4)

Leeks are members of the onion family and are a wonderful accompaniment to fish and shellfish. Try to purchase the smallest leeks you can find, as they will be the most tender.

10 sheets filo (see page 111)
4 tablespoons unsalted butter, melted
1/2 pound bay shrimp
1 small leek, sliced
2 sprigs fresh dill, minced, or 1/2 teaspoon dried dill
3 eggs
1-1/2 cups whipping cream
1/2 teaspoon salt

Preheat the oven to 350 degrees.

Brush the bottom and sides of a round 9-inch baking dish with butter. Place one sheet of filo in the dish and brush with butter. Continue this process until you have layered all the sheets of filo in the dish. With kitchen scissors trim the edge of the filo so that it is 2 inches above the top of the quiche top. Fold the top inch of the filo back over itself towards the inside of the quiche leaving an inch of filo rising above the top of the dish. Brush the folded edge of the filo with butter to seal it against the inside of the filo pastry.

Place the shrimp, leeks and dill on top of the filo. Pour the cream and egg mixture over the shrimp.

Bake the quiche for 30 minutes or until the blade of a knife inserted in the center comes out clean. Let set for 5 - 10 minutes before serving.

Entrées

BROILED JACK (SALMON OR STEELHEAD) WITH PESTO   (Serves 3)

Jacks are young male salmon or steelhead, usually one or two years of age, that are caught occasionally in the ocean or in streams.

4 pounds jack salmon, cut into fillets
Salt and pepper
1 tablespoon pesto (see recipe below)
3/4 cup mayonnaise

Preheat the oven to broil. Set the wire rack 4 inches from the broiler.

Sprinkle salt and freshly ground pepper over the flesh of the fish fillets. Place the salmon on a broiling pan with the flesh side down. Broil for 5 minutes, then turn and broil for 2 more minutes with the skin side down.

While the fish is cooking, mix together the pesto and mayonnaise. After the fish has cooked for 7 minutes, spread the pesto-mayonnaise mixture on the fish fillets and broil for 2 more minutes. The total cooking time will be about 9 minutes, depending on the size of the fish.

Pesto

1-1/2 cups mild olive oil
3-1/2 cups fresh basil leaves
1/2 pound Parmesan cheese, freshly grated
5 cloves garlic
Salt to taste

Purée all of the ingredients together in a food processor or blender until the mixture is homogenous, about 1 minute. Store in a covered jar in the refrigerator.

GRILLED SALMON FILLETS WITH TARRAGON BUTTER (Serves 8)

In early spring, chinook (also called king) salmon start working their way up the rivers from the ocean to spawn. The following recipe is an old method of cooking salmon and can be used for many different types of fish, such as steelhead and large brook trout. It is simple to prepare, beautiful to serve and absolutely the finest tasting fish you will ever eat. If you have alder trees nearby, cut a few green twigs and toss them on the coals the last 10 minutes of the cooking time. It adds a delicate and subtle smoky flavor to the fillets.

1 onion, chopped
1/4 cup parsley, chopped
1 cup butter
Juice of 1 lemon
1-1/2 teaspoons fresh tarragon, minced, or
 1/2 teaspoon whole tarragon, dried and crushed
1 8- to 10-pound chinook salmon, cut into two fillets
Salt and pepper to taste

Place the onion, parsley, butter, lemon juice and tarragon in a small sauce pan and cook over low heat until the onions are tender, about 20 minutes.

Sprinkle salt and pepper on the salmon fillets. Place them on the grill over moderately hot coals, meat side down. Cook for 15 minutes.

Carefully turn the fish over and generously ladle the lemon-butter sauce over the fillets. Arrange the onions in a single layer on top of the salmon. Cook for another 10 minutes, basting often. The fish only needs to be turned once during the cooking process.

Serve the grilled fish topped with the onions on a warm platter garnished with slices of lemon and sprigs of fresh parsley.

Note: You can also wrap the fish entirely in foil and cook following the above recipe. Leave the foil open the last 10 minutes of cooking time. It is easier to handle this way but you will not get the same flavor as you would cooking the fish directly over the coals.

BROILED SALMON STEAKS WITH LIME BUTTER AND FRESH HERBS   (Serves 4)

This recipe can also be used for the barbecue.

8 tablespoons butter
Juice of 1 lime
1 teaspoon fresh chives, minced
1 teaspoon fresh tarragon, minced, or 1/3 teaspoon dried tarragon, crushed
4 salmon steaks cut 3/4 inch thick

Preheat the oven to broil. Place the wire rack 4 inches from the broiler.

Melt the butter in a small saucepan and add the lime juice and minced herbs.

Place the salmon steaks on a broiler pan and brush them liberally with the butter mixture. Cook the steaks 6 minutes on each side, brushing them often with the herb butter.

Serve on a warmed platter garnished with fresh lime slices. Photo page 75.

FETTUCINE RUELLE   (Serves 3 - 4)

This dish was named after a wonderful restaurant I dined in while I was in New York several years ago. I have tried to re-create their fine tasting fettucine with smoked salmon.

2 cups cream
2 tablespoons lemon juice
1 tablespoon capers
1/2 pound spinach fettucine, cooked
6 ounces smoked salmon, shredded
3 sprigs parsley, minced
Salt and pepper to taste
1/2 cup grated Parmesan cheese

Warm a large serving bowl.
Place the cream, lemon juice and capers in a heavy, non-aluminum pot. Cook the sauce mixture over medium heat until the cream begins to thicken slightly, about 10 minutes.
Place the fettucine, sauce, salmon and parsley in the warmed bowl and toss. Season with salt and pepper to taste. Serve directly from the bowl at the table accompanied with Parmesan cheese. Photo page 75.

Entrées

WHOLE SALMON POACHED AND CHILLED (Serves 16)

Salmon poached and served chilled with an herb mayonnaise is not only fantastic to look at, but it is also incredibly delicious. Decorate it with thin slices of cucumber to resemble scales and garnish the fish with edible flowers from your garden, letting your imagination be your guide.

    1 poached 8- to 10-pound salmon, completely chilled (see page 18)
    1 recipe herb mayonnaise (see page 131)
    2 English cucumbers, thinly sliced
    1 bunch fresh dill
    1 bunch parsley
    2 heads green curly lettuce, mustard greens, or 5 to 6 sword ferns; a few fresh flower blossoms (nasturtiums, daisies or pansies)
    6 lemon slices
    1 pitted black olive

Remove the head and tail with a sharp knife if you are going to use a fish board with a metal head and tail. Leave the head but remove the tail if you are going to serve the fish on a large platter. Carefully remove the skin from the top side of the poached salmon.

Line the serving dish with lettuce leaves and place the salmon on it. Spread an even layer of the herb mayonnaise over the entire fish. Overlap the cucumbers on the top side of the fish to resemble fish scales. Cut the olive in half and use it for an eye if you have left the head intact. Make a dramatic tail by using 5 to 6 sprigs of fresh dill and sticking them under the tail end of the fish.

Garnish with lemon slices, sprigs of parsley and the flower blossoms. Keep the fish in the refrigerator until you are ready to serve it.

STEELHEAD POACHED IN BEER   (Serves 4)

I would like to dedicate this recipe to my brother-in-law, Lee, who helps to keep my larder stocked with steelhead throughout the year and who keeps his ice chest well-stocked with beer for those memorable float trips down Oregon's Deschutes River.

2 pounds steelhead steaks
4 slices lime
4 slices onion
1 12-ounce can beer, less several sips
Salt and freshly ground pepper
1/2 pint heavy cream

Preheat the oven to 375 degrees.

Place the fish in a baking dish. Put a slice of lime and a slice of onion on each steak. Add the beer to the baking dish and a sprinkling of salt and freshly ground pepper.

Bake the fish uncovered for 12 to 15 minutes or until the fish flakes. Remove the fish to a warmed platter.

Add the cream to the cooking juices and cook over high heat until it slightly thickens, about 5 minutes. Season with salt and pepper and pour the sauce over the fish.

Entrées

POACHED STEELHEAD WITH PANCETTA AND ROSEMARY   (Serves 4)

Pancetta is a type of cured Italian meat similar to American bacon. It is made from the pork belly which is rolled and seasoned and it is delicious. It can be purchased at most delicatessens but if you are unable to find it substitute bacon instead.

2 ounces pancetta, cut into 1/2-inch pieces
1 teaspoon whole rosemary (dried or fresh)
1-1/2 pounds fresh steelhead; fillet and cut into four 6-ounce pieces
Salt and freshly ground pepper
1/2 cup dry white wine
1 heaping tablespoon butter
1 teaspoon parsley, minced

In a heavy skillet brown the pancetta over medium-high heat. With a slotted spoon remove the pancetta to a small plate and discard the remaining fat.

Wipe out the pan with a paper towel. Place the pan back on the burner and sprinkle the bottom of the pan with 1/2 teaspoon of rosemary. Add the fillets and season with a dash of salt and some freshly ground pepper. Crush the remaining 1/2 teaspoon of rosemary and evenly distribute it over the steelhead. Pour the wine over all and cover the pan with a lid.

Cook for 5 minutes or until the fish flakes with a fork. Remove the fish to a warmed platter. Add the butter and cooked pancetta to the pan and when the butter melts, divide it equally over the fillets. Sprinkle with chopped parsley and serve immediately. Photo page 76.

STURGEON PROVENCALE (Serves 8)

When food is cooked "provençale" it will generally contain garlic, olive oil and tomatoes. All of these ingredients are characteristic of the cooking in Provence, a region in southern France, where this term originated.

    2 tablespoons olive oil
    2 shallots, peeled and chopped or 2 chopped green onions
    1 large onion, chopped
    4 fresh tomatoes, peeled, seeded and chopped
        or
    1 15-ounce can whole tomatoes, drained and chopped
    1/2 teaspoon whole thyme, crushed
    1 bunch fresh spinach, washed
    2 tablespoons heavy cream
    8 sturgeon steaks
    Salt and pepper
    Juice of 1 lemon

Preheat the oven to 350 degrees.

Chop the shallots and onions and sauté them in a small amount of olive oil until they start to turn brown, about 8 - 10 minutes. Add the tomatoes and thyme and cook until the tomatoes are tender, about 5 more minutes.

Cook the spinach over high heat for 2 - 3 minutes. Drain and purée in a food processor or blender with the cream until smooth. Season with salt and pepper to taste.

Sprinkle the fish steaks with salt, pepper and fresh lemon juice. Spread a thin layer of the purée of spinach on each fillet. Place the steaks in a greased baking dish and gently spoon the tomato mixture and juices over the top. Bake, uncovered, for 20 - 25 minutes. Photo page 77.

Entrées

BAKED FILLET OF SOLE WITH BROCCOLI (Serves 4)

The following white sauce can be made several days ahead of time if you keep it covered in the refrigerator. Buy the fish fresh the day you are going to serve them.

3 tablespoons butter
3 tablespoons flour
2 cups milk
1/3 cup white wine
1/3 cup Parmesan cheese plus 2 tablespoons
1-1/2 pounds fillet of sole
1/2 pound broccoli, trimmed and blanched

Preheat the oven to 350 degrees.
Heat the butter in a saucepan and stir in the flour. Cook over medium heat for 3 minutes stirring constantly. Add the milk and wine and stir the mixture constantly until it thickens. Stir 1/3 cup of Parmesan cheese and season with salt and pepper.
Butter an 8-by-11-inch baking dish.
Lay each fillet on a flat surface and sprinkle it with salt and pepper. Place 1/2 teaspoon of butter in the center of the fillet and roll it up lengthwise. Place the rolled fillets in the center of the baking dish and surround them with the pieces of broccoli. Pour the sauce over all and sprinkle with 2 tablespoons Parmesan cheese. Cover with foil and bake for 25 minutes or until they flake when tested with a fork.

Microwave directions: Microwave on high for 1-1/2 - 2 minutes.

FILLET OF SOLE WITH CURRY   (Serves 4)

Curry powder is a blend of many spices and the best kind to use is that which you make yourself. If you do not have time to make your own, Sharwood's Curry Powder is a good brand to buy.

3 tablespoons butter
1/3 cup flour
2 teaspoons curry powder
1-1/2 pounds fillet of sole
4 lemon slices
Salt and pepper to taste

Heat the butter in a large skillet.

Mix the flour and curry powder together in a shallow bowl and dip each fillet in the flour mixture. Place the coated fillets in the hot butter and cook for 3 - 4 minutes a side or until they are done. Season with salt and pepper.

Serve the cooked fillets on warmed plates sprinkled with fresh lemon juice.

Entrées

DEEP-FRIED SQUID IN BEER BATTER (Serves 4)

This versatile batter can be used for any medium- to firm-fleshed fish.

2 pounds whole Pacific squid, cleaned and cut into rings*
1-1/2 cups flour
1 can beer
Pinch of salt
1 cup safflower oil
Tartar sauce (see page 131)

Make the beer batter by mixing together 1 cup of flour with the beer and a pinch of salt. Let it sit at room temperature for 2 hours.

Place the remaining cup of flour on a sheet of wax paper and lightly dust the pieces of squid in it.

Heat the oil in a heavy, deep skillet. Dredge the squid in the batter, then cook in the hot oil until golden brown on both sides, about 45 seconds. Drain on pieces of paper towel. Serve with homemade tartar sauce.

*To clean squid, the West Coast Fisheries Development Foundation recommends the following method: holding mantle (body) in one hand, pinch pen (transparent backbone) with index finger and thumb of opposite hand, separating pen from mantle. Gently pull pen out of mantle, easing viscera out along with pen. Cut away tentacles. Scrape membrane to loosen from mantle. Pull away all membrane and discard. Rinse mantle thoroughly with cold water to remove any remaining viscera; pat dry with paper towels. Cut into rings. (The tentacles can also be used in the recipe.)

Variation: Substitute 1-1/2 pounds of shark fillets, cut into 1-inch squares, in place of the squid.

TROUT STUFFED WITH SMOKED SALMON   (Serves 4)

A favorite way to cook fresh trout is to stuff them with smoked salmon, roll them in cornmeal and fry them on a hot griddle. I like to prepare the griddle by sautéeing two onions in equal amounts of butter and bacon grease before I cook the fish. I push the onions to one side when I am ready to cook the fish.

- 1-1/2 tablespoons butter
- 1-1/2 tablespoons bacon grease
- 2 yellow onions, peeled and sliced
- 1/2 cup cornmeal
- 4 - 6 trout, cleaned
- 1/4 pound smoked salmon, broken up into bite-sized pieces

Heat the butter and bacon grease on a griddle. Add the onions and cook until they are soft and golden brown. Shove them to one end of the griddle.

Stuff the trout with the smoked salmon and roll each fish in the cornmeal. Place the trout on the hot griddle and cook 3 - 5 minutes a side or until the meat flakes when tested with a fork.

Entrées

MINT-STUFFED RAINBOW TROUT   (Serves 2 - 3)

If you are unable to locate fresh mint for this recipe, substitute fresh parsley, basil or dill.

**4 medium-sized rainbow trout
4 sprigs fresh mint
Salt and pepper
4 slices red onion, peeled
1 cup sour cream
Juice of 1/2 lime**

Preheat the oven to 350 degrees.

Lay the fish in a small greased baking dish. Pull the mint leaves off their stems and lay them inside the fish cavities. Sprinkle with salt and freshly ground pepper. Lay the onion slices on top of the fish.

Mix the sour cream with the lime juice and pour the mixture over the fish. Cover with foil and bake until the fish flakes when tested with a fork, about 25 minutes. Garnish with fresh mint and lime slices.

Variation: Substitute true cod, halibut or lingcod in place of the trout. Place the mint leaves on the bottom of the greased baking dish. Lay the fish pieces on top and follow the above recipe. Photo page 78.

PAN-FRIED TROUT WITH FRESH FENNEL   (Serves 4)

Fennel is an herb which you would probably recognize most from the unique flavor its seeds give Italian sausages. The feathery leaves of this unique plant go well with fish and its bulb can be sliced, sautéed in butter and served as an accompaniment.

2 tablespoons bacon grease
2 tablespoons safflower oil
8 fresh trout, cleaned
1/2 cup cornmeal
8 sprigs fresh fennel
Juice of 1/2 lemon

Place the grease and oil in a large frying pan. Roll the trout in the cornmeal and give them a gentle shake to remove the excess. Place a sprig of fennel in each trout and fry them until the outside skin is slightly crisp and the meat flakes when tested with a fork, about 10 minutes. Arrange the fish on a warmed platter and add the lemon juice to the pan. Scrape the pan well and pour the liquid over the fish.

Stocks

A fish stock is a liquid that is made by simmering fish bones with aromatic vegetables, herbs and spices. Stocks are then used as a base for fish sauces. Unlike chicken or beef stock, fish stock is cooked for a very short period of time.

The best fish bones to use in a stock are from mild-flavored fish with a low fat content, such as halibut or flounder. Call your favorite fish market ahead of time to order fish bones for stock if you know you are going to need them. There should be no skin attached to the bones; otherwise your stock will be an unappetizing gray color.

Most fish stocks are seasoned with a variety of ingredients. Be careful not to get carried away with bay leaf, celery or green pepper. All of them are very powerful and can overpower any subtle flavors that the fish bones may have imparted to the stock.

Bottled clam juice can be used in place of fish stock if you do not have time to make your own, but I recommend trying several different brands to see which one you like best. Most of them have a high salt content so be careful not to oversalt your stock. Season the finished sauce with salt and pepper just before it is to be served instead of salting the fish stock.

FISH STOCK   (Makes 1 quart)

    2 pounds fish bones
    1 small onion, peeled and cut into eighths
    1 carrot, cut into quarters
    1 stick of celery, cut into quarters
    1/4 teaspoon whole thyme, crushed
    1 cup dry white wine
    1 quart water

Place all of the above ingredients into a deep, non-aluminum saucepan and bring to a boil. Immediately turn the heat down and simmer the liquid for 30 minutes. Cool and strain.

COURT BOUILLON
(Makes enough to poach a 10-pound fish)

Court bouillion is a term of French origin and it refers to an aromatic liquid that is used to cook fish. This is the liquid I use to poach salmon or steelhead.

    3 quarts water
    4 cups dry white wine
    1 onion, quartered
    2 cloves garlic, crushed
    1/2 cup fresh parsley, chopped
    1 teaspoon whole thyme, crushed
    1/2 teaspoon whole tarragon, crushed
    1 bay leaf, broken in half
    1 tablespoon salt
    20 peppercorns
    1 whole lemon, sliced

In a non-aluminum pan combine all of the above ingredients. Bring them to a boil, then reduce the heat to simmer. Cook for 1 hour.

Sauces

Most fish and shellfish have a mild flavor and the addition of a sauce — whether hot or cold — makes a nice complement to cooked fillets, steaks or whole fish. Grilled, sautéed or poached fish are usually sauced after they have been cooked, while fish cooked in the oven are often baked in a sauce.

Cookware for sauces should be heavy-bottomed enamel, stainless steel, Pyrex, porcelain or tin-lined copper. Aluminum should not be used because sauces can be discolored by the addition of any acid, such as wine or vinegar, or by egg yolks.

LEMON BUTTER

Lemon butter is the simplest of all the fish sauces, requiring only two ingredients: lemon and butter, but it provides a tasty sauce for dunking fresh shellfish.

8 tablespoons butter
2 teaspoons fresh lemon juice

Heat the butter until it melts and add the lemon juice. Serve warm in individual small bowls.

LIME BUTTER

Follow the recipe for lemon butter except substitute lime juice for the lemon juice. During the summer months limes are much cheaper than lemons and they provide a pleasant change from the ubiquitous lemon that one always thinks of with fish.

MAYONNAISE

Homemade mayonnaise is simple to make if you have a food processor or blender and it tastes so much better than what you can buy commercially. Mix enough of this mayonnaise with any cooked fish or shellfish to bind it together. It can then be used as a spread for sandwiches.

1 whole egg
1 teaspoon red wine vinegar
1/2 teaspoon salt
1-1/2 cups safflower oil

Place all of the ingredients except the oil in the bowl of a food processor or blender. Blend for 30 seconds and, with the machine still running, slowly add the oil until the mixture gradually thickens.

LEMON MAYONNAISE

Serve this sauce with cold, cooked shellfish.

1 whole egg
1 teaspoon fresh lemon juice
1/2 teaspoon grated lemon rind
3 tablespoons chives, chopped
1/2 teaspoon salt
1-1/2 cups safflower oil

Place all of the ingredients except the oil in the bowl of a food processor or blender. Blend for 30 seconds then, with the machine still running, slowly add the oil until the mixture gradually thickens.

HERB MAYONNAISE

Serve this mayonnaise with chilled, cooked shellfish.

1 whole egg
1 teaspoon wine vinegar
1/2 teaspoon salt
1 clove garlic, peeled
3 tablespoons parsley, chopped
3 tablespoons scallions, chopped
1-1/2 cups mild olive oil

Place all of the ingredients except the oil in the bowl of a food processor or blender. Blend for 30 seconds, then, with the machine still running, slowly add the oil until the mixture gradually thickens.

TARTAR SAUCE

Capers are the small, unopened buds of flowers that grow on a shrub found in Europe. They have a slightly bitter taste which is a nice contrast to the mild flavor of most fish. Serve this sauce with any shellfish or any sautéed fish.

1 cup sour cream
1/2 cup mayonnaise
1 tablespoon capers
1 teaspoon lemon juice
1 teaspoon fresh dill, chopped, or
   1/2 teaspoon dried dill
1 teaspoon fresh parsley, chopped
Salt and white pepper

Mix all of the ingredients together. Season with salt and pepper to taste.

SAUCE MEUNIÈRE

Make this simple sauce in the same pan in which you have sautéed sole, trout, lingcod, oysters or clams.

Juice of 1/2 lemon
2 tablespoons butter
1 teaspoon capers (optional)
1/2 teaspoon parsley, chopped

Remove the cooked fish to a warmed platter. Place the skillet back on the burner and add the butter, lemon juice and capers. While the butter heats, scrape the cooked particles off the bottom of the pan with a wooden spoon and mix them with the butter. When the sauce is hot, pour it over the fish and garnish with chopped parsley.

SAUCE PROVENÇALE

This sauce goes well with sturgeon, sole and frog legs.

2 shallots, peeled and chopped
1 large onion, chopped
2 tablespoons olive oil
4 fresh tomatoes, peeled, seeded and chopped, or
   1 15-ounce can whole tomatoes, drained and chopped
1/2 teaspoon whole thyme, crushed
Salt and pepper to taste

Sauté the onions and shallots in the olive oil until they start to turn brown, about 8 - 10 minutes. Add the tomatoes, and thyme and cook until the tomatoes are tender, about 5 more minutes. Season with salt and pepper to taste.

HOLLANDAISE SAUCE

This classic French sauce could make pieces of sliced cardboard taste heavenly. If you have either a blender or food processor it is very simple to make. If you do not have either machine you will need a wire sauce whisk to incorporate the butter into the other ingredients. This sauce goes well with almost any poached fish.

2 egg yolks
1-1/2 teaspoons lemon juice
Pinch salt
Pinch cayenne pepper
1 tablespoon hot water
8 tablespoons hot melted butter

Rinse the bowl of a food processor or blender out with hot water and dry it with a dish towel. Place all the ingredients except the butter in the work bowl and turn the machine on. With the machine still running slowly add the melted butter and the mixture will gradually thicken. Serve immediately or store in a warmed thermos until it is needed.

SEAFOOD COCKTAIL SAUCE

This simple-to-prepare cocktail sauce can be used to accompany cooked shellfish or oysters on the half shell.

1/2 cup prepared cocktail sauce
1/2 cup homemade tomato sauce
1 teaspoon fresh lemon juice
1 teaspoon prepared horseradish
Salt and freshly ground pepper to taste

Mix all ingredients together in a mixing bowl. Photo page 80.

MOUSSELINE SAUCE

Once you have mastered Hollandaise sauce, this sauce becomes very simple to make. Serve it with poached or baked salmon.

> 1-1/2 cups Hollandaise sauce (see preceding page)
> 1-1/2 cups whipped cream

Mix the whipped cream and the Hollandaise sauce together in a double boiler. Gently heat the mixture over hot water, stirring constantly. It must never be allowed to boil. Serve immediately.

CREAMY MUSHROOM SAUCE

Use either the commercially grown white mushroom or, if you can find them, chanterelle mushrooms.

> 3 tablespoons of butter
> 1 shallot, peeled and chopped
>   or
> 1 tablespoon chopped green onion
> 1/2 pound fresh mushrooms, cleaned and sliced vertically
> 1/2 cup fish stock (optional)
> 1 cup heavy cream

Heat the butter in a sauté pan and add the chopped shallot. Cook for 5 minutes or until the shallot pieces start to brown. Add the mushrooms and cook them over medium heat until they start to soften. Pour the cream and fish stock over the mushrooms and shallot mixture and cook the sauce until it thickens, about 10 minutes.

Smoking Fish

There is nothing more delectable than a piece of hickory-smoked chinook salmon or a flavorful chunk of smoked black cod, and it is always such a satisfying feeling to serve them to guests after having smoked them yourself!

Smoking fish is a simple task with only four basic steps. After the fish is thoroughly cleaned, it must be soaked in a salt solution called a brine. The salt draws water out of the fish and at the same time enters into the fish's flesh. This speeds the smoking process and decreases the chances of spoilage.

After the fish has soaked in the brine for two or three hours, it needs to be rinsed in several changes of fresh water for 15 - 20 minutes to rid the fish of excess salt. The fish is then air-dried for several hours which leaves a thin layer of dissolved proteins on the surface of the fish called a "pellicule." The pellicule is what gives the fish a glossy appearance after it has been smoked.

The final step is to actually smoke the fish and either a hot- or cold-smoke can be used. I use a Little Chief Smoker that hot-smokes the fish between 150 - 200 degrees. Hot-smoking is also called "smoke cooking" and the fish is placed in a smoker with a temperature range of 120 - 225 degrees. It is smoked until the fish is cooked and has reached the degree of dryness you prefer. When this method is used, the fish is also cooked as well as being smoked. Fish that has been prepared in this manner is often sold in fish markets as "kippered."

Cold-smoking is usually done in a smoker with temperatures below 120 degrees. The smoky flavor is imparted into the flesh of the fish and the cooking process takes place very slowly over a period of three or four days.

One way to speed up this process is to cold-smoke the fish for 8 hours to give the fish a smoky flavor and then complete the cooking process in the oven. The fish can be wrapped in foil and placed in a 325-degree oven until it flakes with a fork and its internal temperature is 167 degrees.

I prefer to smoke my fish with a mixture of hickory and alder chips which can be purchased prepackaged at most sporting goods stores. The smoke from the chips not only provides a savory flavor, but it also acts as a preservative. Aldehydes and ketones, chemicals found in the smoke, penetrate the flesh of the fish and help to inhibit the growth of bacteria. Generally, only wood from hardwood trees is used for smoking because non-deciduous trees (those that do not lose their leaves) give off a bitter tasting resin.

The best fish to smoke are those with the highest fat content, such as salmon, black cod, trout, smelt, herring, steelhead and catfish. The brine and the technique are the same for all of the fish and only the smoking time will vary due to the thickness of the fish being smoked.

Smaller fish, such as smelt, herring and small trout, can be smoked whole. They need to be cleaned and the heads removed before being placed in the brine. Larger fish, after they have been cleaned and decapitated, should be cut up into fillets and then into 2-inch-wide sections. Leave the skin intact and smoke the fish skin side down.

Smoking fish is not an exact art. Your results will vary with outside seasonal temperatures, the type of fish smoked and the thickness of the fish or pieces of fish. For these reasons, it is important to keep a good record of your smoking ventures. As with anything, the more you do it, the better you become at it. Trial and error is the only way to learn and by keeping good records you will quickly be able to master this ancient method of preserving fish.

MASTER RECIPE FOR SMOKED FISH

This recipe can be used for any fish you wish to smoke. Use either fresh fish or frozen fish that has been thawed in the refrigerator. Salmon, steelhead and other large fish should be cut into 2-by-3-inch pieces while smaller fish, such as smelt and small trout, can be eviscerated, decapitated and smoked whole. This recipe makes enough brine to soak 3 pounds of fish.

Brine

> 1/2 cup salt
> 1 quart water
> 3 tablespoons cracked pepper (optional)
> 1/2 cup sugar (optional)
> 3 pounds of fish, ready to be smoked

Mix the salt, water, pepper and sugar together in a shallow bowl. Place the fish in the brine and soak it for a minimum of 3 hours. Turn the fish every 1/2 hour while it soaks.

Remove the fish from the brine and place it in a bowl of fresh water for 10 minutes.

Place the fish on a wire rack to air-dry. Smaller fish will dry in 4 hours while larger fish will dry in 8 hours.

Put the fish in the smoker. If you are going to smoke small pieces of fish, do not crowd them on the smoking racks. There should be an inch of space between each piece of fish.

Smoke smaller fish for about 4 hours and larger fish for 8 to 12 hours. Use at least 4 pan loads of chips during the smoking process. The fish is done when it no longer looks raw and flakes easily. Oftentimes it is necessary to cut into the thickest part of the fish to visually check for doneness.

Smoked fish can be kept in the refrigerator for a month and frozen for up to three months. After three months in the freezer, the quality of the fish rapidly declines.

RECORD FOR SMOKING FISH

Date	Type Fish	Weight	Type Cure	Length Cure	Type Fuel	Total Hours	Notes

Bibliography

Browning, Robert J. *Fisheries of the North Pacific*, Anchorage, 1974.
Charley, Helen. *Food Science*, New York, 1971.
De Carli, Franco. *The World of Fish*, New York, 1974.
Eschmeyer, William N. *A Field Guide to Pacific Coast Fishes of North America*, Boston, 1983.
Hewlett K. Gilbey and Hewlett Stefani. *Sea Life of the Pacific Northwest*, Canada, 1976.
Lusch, E. A. *How to Catch and Identify the Gamefish of Oregon*, Portland, 1978.
McClane, J. *The Encyclopedia of Fish Cookery*, New York, 1977.
Netboy, Anthony. *Salmon of the Pacific Northwest*, Portland, Oregon, 1958.
Netboy, Anthony. *The Salmon: Their Fight for Survival*, Boston, 1974.
"Oyster Culture, A Natural Resource Revived," Seattle, 1967.
"Pacific Northwest Marine Fishes," Washington State Department of Fisheries, Olympia, 1967.
"Razor Clams," Oregon Fish Commission, Educational Bulletin No. 4, Portland, 1963.
The Audubon Society Field Guide to North American Fishes, Whales and Dolphins, New York, 1983.
"The Bay Clams of Oregon," Oregon Fish Commission, Educational Bulletin No. 2, Portland, 1958.
Wheeler, Jacqueline D., and Hebard, Chieko E., eds., *Seafood Products Resource Guide*, Virginia, 1980.

Index

ABALONE
  How to cook, 15, 16
  Abalone Baked in its Shell, 92
ALBACORE
  General information, 21
  How to buy, 21
  How to cook, 21
APPETIZERS
  Antipasto Basket with Herb Mayonnaise, 42
  Cream Cheese and Caviar, 52
  Clams Stuffed with Dungeness Crab and Cream Cheese, 44
  Humboldt County Clam Dip, 45
  Crab Pâte, 47
  Crab Cocktail with Avocado Dressing, 50
  Crayfish Cooked with Fresh Dill, 48
  Gravlax, 53
  Mussels with Garlic Butter, 46
  Smoked Oyster Spread, 55
  Artichoke Hearts Stuffed with Smoked Salmon, 49
  Broiled Scallops Wrapped in Pancetta, 51
  Shrimp Butter, 47
  Shrimp and Green Onion in Red Pepper Boats, 54
  Molded Shrimp Appetizer, 56
  Curried Tuna, 43
BLACK COD (see SABLEFISH)
BAKING, 15
BROILING, 16
CATFISH
  Catfish Parmesan with a Coulis of Tomato, 93
  Catfish Meunière, 94
CAVIAR
  Cream Cheese and Caviar, 52
CLAMS
  Humboldt County Clam Dip, 45
  Butter (Quahog, Beefsteak, Washington, Coney Island, Great Oregon), 25
  General Information, 25
  How to cook, 25
  Clams Stuffed with Dungeness Crab and Cream Cheese, 44
  Creamy Clam Chowder, 89
  Geoduck
    General information, 25
    How to buy, 26
    How to cook, 26
    Creamy Clam Chowder, 89
  Horseneck (Gaper, Blue, Empire)
    General information, 25
    How to cook, 25
    Creamy Clam Chowder, 89
  Littleneck

  General information, 24
  How to buy, 25
  How to cook, 25
  Steamer Clams Cooked with Garlic and Rosemary, 100
  Bouillabaisse, 86
  Dungeness Crab and Clam Cioppino, 84
  Razor
    General information, 25
    How to buy, 24
    How to cook, 24
    Quick-Fried Razor Clams, 99
COD
  General information, 26
  True (Pacific, gray), 26
    General information, 26
    How to buy, 26
    How to cook, 26
    True Cod with Sour Cream and Mint (Variation), 125
COURT BOUILLON
  General information, 128
  How to cook, 128
CRAB
  Blue (soft shell), 21
  Dungeness
    General information, 21
    How to buy, 22
    How to cook, 22
    Bouillabaisse, 86
    Crab and Clam Cioppino, 84
    Clams Stuffed with Dungeness Crab and Cream Cheese, 44
    Crab Pâte, 47
    Molded Crab Appetizer, 56
    Crab Cocktail with Avocado Dressing, 50
    Fresh Mushroom and Spinach Salad with Crab Legs, 57
    Curried Crab on Beefsteak Tomato Slices, 58
    Cream of Crab Bisque with Mushrooms and Sherry, 85
    Hot Dungeness Crab with Spicy Ginger Sauce, 96
    Sautéed Crab Meat Patties, 98
    Fresh Crab with Purée of Leek Au Gratin, 95
    Crab Legs Sautéed in Madeira and Brandy, 97
  King
    General information, 21
    How to buy, 22
    Bouillabaisse, 86
CRAYFISH
  General information, 27
  How to buy, 27
  How to cook, 27
  Crayfish Cooked with Fresh

  Dill, 48
  Bouillabaisse, 86
DOVER SOLE
  General information, 28
  How to buy, 28
  How to cook, 28
ENGLISH SOLE
  General information, 28
  How to buy, 28
  How to cook, 28
ENTRÉES
  Abalone Baked in its Shell, 92
  Catfish Meunière, 94
  Catfish Parmesan with a Coulis of Tomato, 93
  Steamer Clams Cooked with Garlic and Rosemary, 100
  Quick-Fried Razor Clams, 99
  Hot Dungeness Crab with Spicy Ginger Sauce, 96
  Sautéed Crab Meat Patties, 98
  Fresh Crab with Purée of Leek Au Gratin, 95
  Crab Legs Sautéed in Madeira and Brandy, 97
  Halibut and Proscuitto with Shisk Kebabs, 101
  Teriyaki Lingcod with Fresh Ginger, 102
  Baked Perch with Sour Cream and Chiles, 104
  Skate Wings with Lemon Butter and Capers, 107
  Garlicky Jumbo Shrimp, 109
  Shrimp Poached in White Wine, 108
  Wholewheat Crêpes Stuffed with Shrimp and Sour Cream, 110
  Leek and Shrimp Quiche with Fresh Dill, 112
  Shrimp Baked in Filo, 111
  Sautéed Sablefish with Salsa, 105
  Broiled Jack Salmon with Pesto, 113
  Grilled Salmon Fillets with Tarragon Butter, 114
  Broiled Salmon Steaks with Lime Butter and Fresh Herbs, 115
  Fettucine Ruelle, 116
  Whole Salmon Poached and Chilled, 117
  Steelhead Poached in Beer, 118
  Poached Steelhead with Pancetta and Rosemary, 119
  Sturgeon Provençale, 120
  Fillet of Sole with Curry, 122
  Baked Fillet of Sole with Broccoli, 121
  Deep-Fried Squid in Beer Batter, 123

140

Mint-Stuffed Rainbow Trout, 125
Trout Stuffed with Smoked
    Salmon, 124
Pan-Fried Trout with Fresh
    Fennel, 126
Oysters Florentine, 103
**FLATFISH (see DOVER SOLE,
    FLOUNDER, HALIBUT,
    PETRALE SOLE, REX SOLE,
    SANDDABS, TURBOT)**
**FILLET OF SOLE (see Dover
    SOLE, PETRALE SOLE,
    ENGLISH SOLE)**
Fillet of Sole with Curry, 122
Baked Fillet of Sole with
    Broccoli, 121
Sole Parmesan with a Coulis of
    Tomato (Variation), 93
FISH STOCK, 128
**FLOUNDER (see DOVER SOLE,
    ENGLISH SOLE, HALIBUT,
    PETRALE SOLE, REX SOLE,
    SANDDABS, TURBOT)**
GRAVLAX
Basic recipe, 53
GREENLING (see LINGCOD)
GRILLING, 16
HALIBUT
General information, 29
How to buy, 29
How to cook, 29
Halibut and Proscuitto Shish
    Kebabs, 101
Bouillabaisse, 86
Halibut with Sour Cream and
    Mint (Variation), 125
LINGCOD
General information, 30
How to buy, 30
How to cook, 30
Teriyaki Lingcod with Fresh
    Ginger, 102
Lingcod with Sour Cream and
    Mint (Variation), 125
LOX
Lox, Capers and Marinated
    Onions on Butter Lettuce, 81
MACKEREL (see ALBACORE)
MICROWAVING, 19
MUSSELS
General information, 30
How to buy, 31
How to cook, 31
Bouillabaisse, 86
Mussel Bisque with Saffron, 88
Mussels with Garlic Butter, 46
Blue (edible)
    General information, 30
California
    General information, 30
Smoked Mussels
    General information, 31
    How to buy, 31
    Antipasto Basket with Herb
        Mayonnaise, 42
    Smoked Mussel Bisque, 87
OYSTERS
General information, 32
How to buy, 33
How to cook, 32
Oyster Stew, 90
Oysters Florentine, 103
Pacific
    General information, 32
Willapa (Olympia)
    General information, 32

PACIFIC COD (see COD)
**PACIFIC FLOUNDER (see
    FLOUNDER)**
PERCH
General information, 33
How to buy, 33
How to cook, 33
Baked Perch with Sour Cream
    and Chiles, 104
PETRALE SOLE
General information, 28
How to buy, 28
How to cook, 28
Baked Fillet of Sole with
    Broccoli, 121
Fillet of Sole with Curry, 122
POACHING, 118
**PRAWNS (see SHRIMP, Medium
    and Large)**
RED SNAPPER (Pacific Snapper)
General information, 33
How to buy, 33
How to cook, 33
REX SOLE
General information, 29
How to buy, 29
How to cook, 29
**ROCKFISH (see PERCH, PACIFIC
    SNAPPER)**
SABLEFISH (Black Cod)
General information, 34
How to buy, 34
How to cook, 34
Bouillabaisse, 86
Sautéed Sablefish with Salsa, 105
SALADS
Fresh Mushroom and Spinach
    Salad with Crab Legs, 57
Curried Crab on Beefsteak
    Tomato Slices, 58
Danish Patato Salad with
    Smoked Chinook Salmon, 59
Lox, Capers and Marinated
    Onions on Butter Lettuce, 81
Rice Salad with Bay Shrimp and
    Fresh Herbs, 82
Tossed Green Salad with Bay
    Shrimp, 63
Minced Shrimp, Celery and Onion
    in a Tangy Vinaigrette, 62
Shrimp Coleslaw, 64
Marinated Cocktail Artichoke
    Salad with Shrimp, 83
Pasta Salad with Pesto and
    Smoked Salmon, 64
Simple Tuna Salad, 60
Salad Nicoise, 61
SALMON
General information, 36
How to Buy, 36
Bouillabaisse, 86
Gravlax, 53
Lox, Capers and Marinated
    Onions on Butter Lettuce, 81
Broiled Jack Salmon with Pesto,
    113
Broiled Salmon Steaks with Lime
    Butter and Fresh Herbs, 115
Grilled Salmon Fillets with
    Tarragon Butter, 114
Whole Salmon Poached and
    Chilled, 117
Chinook
    General information, 36
    How to buy, 37
    How to cook, 38

Chum
    General information, 37
    How to buy, 37
    How to cook, 38
Coho (Silver)
    General information, 37
    How to buy, 38
    How to cook, 37
Pink
    General information, 37
Sockeye
    General information, 37
    How to buy, 38
    How to cook, 37
SANDDABS
General information, 30
How to buy, 30
How to cook, 30
SAUCES
General information, 129
How to make, 129
Seafood Cocktail Sauce, 133
Lemon Butter, 17, 129
Lime Butter, 129
Mayonnaise, 130
Herb Mayonnaise, 43, 131
Lemon Mayonnaise, 130
Tartar, 131
Hollandaise, 133
Meunière, 132
Mousseline, 134
Creamy Mushroom, 134
Provençale, 132
SAUTÉEING, 14
SCALLOPS
General information, 34
How to buy, 35
How to cook, 35
Broiled Scallops Wrapped in
    Pancetta, 51
Scallops Florentine
    (Variation), 103
**SEA-RUN RAINBOW TROUT
    (see TROUT/STEELHEAD)**
SHARK
Deep-Fried Shark in Beer
    Batter (Variation), 123
SHRIMP (Small Pink)
General information, 35
How to buy, 35
Shrimp Butter, 47
Shrimp and Green Onion in Red
    Pepper Boats, 54
Shrimp Cocktail with Avocado
    Dressing, 50
Molded Shrimp Appetizer, 56
Rice Salad with Bay Shrimp, 82
Tossed Green Salad with Cocktail
    Shrimp, 63
Minced Shrimp, Celery and Onion
    in a Tangy Vinaigrette, 62
Shrimp Coleslaw, 64
Tomatoes Stuffed with Shrimp
    (Variation I), 62
Avocado Stuffed with Shrimp
    (Variation II), 62
Wholewheat Crêpes Stuffed with
    Shrimp and Sour Cream, 110
Leek and Shrimp Quiche with
    Fresh Dill, 112
Shrimp Baked in Filo, 111
SHRIMP (Prawn)
General information, 35
How to cook, 35
Antipasto Basket with Herb
    Mayonnaise, 42

141

Shrimp Poached in Wine, 108
Garlicky Jumbo Shrimp, 109
Marinated Cocktail Artichoke
  Salad with Shrimp, 83
Bouillabaisse, 86
SKATE
General information, 38
How to buy, 39
How to cook, 39
Skate Wings with Lemon Butter
  and Capers, 107
SMOKING FISH
General information, 135
Master recipe, 137
SMOKED MUSSELS (see MUSSELS)
Smoked Mussel Bisque, 87
Antipasto Basket with Herb
  Mayonnaise, 42
SMOKED OYSTERS
Smoked Oyster Spread, 55
Antipasto Basket with Herb
  Mayonnaise, 42
SMOKED SALMON
Artichoke Hearts Stuffed with
  Smoked Salmon, 49
Cream of Chanterelle Soup with
  Smoked Salmon, 91
Danish Potato Salad with Smoked
  Chinook Salmon, 59
Fettucine Ruelle (Pasta and
  Smoked Salmon), 116

Pasta Salad with Pesto and
  Smoked Salmon, 64
Molded Smoked Salmon
  Appetizer, 56
SNAPPER (see RED SNAPPER)
SOLES (see FILLET OF SOLE)
SOUPS
Bouillabaisse, 86
Dungeness Crab and Clam
  Cioppino, 84
Creamy Clam Chowder, 89
Cream of Crab Bisque with
  Mushrooms and Sherry, 85
Mussel Bisque with Saffron, 88
Smoked Mussel Bisque, 87
Oyster Stew, 90
Cream of Chanterelle Soup with
  Smoked Salmon, 91
STEAMING, 19
STOCK(Fish)
General information, 127
How to cook, 127
Fish Stock, 128
Court Bouillon, 128
STEELHEAD
(see TROUT/STEELHEAD)
General information, 40
How to cook, 41
Steelhead Poached in Beer, 118
Poached Steelhead with Pancetta
  and Rosemary, 119

Steelhead with Pesto, 113
STURGEON
General information, 39
How to buy, 39
How to cook, 39
Sturgeon Provençale, 120
Bouillabaisse, 86
SWORDFISH
General information, 40
How to buy, 40
How to cook, 40
SQUID
Deep-Fried Squid in Beer Batter, 123
TROUT (see TROUT/STEELHEAD)
General information, 40
How to cook, 41
Pan-Fried Trout with Fresh
  Fennel, 126
Trout Stuffed with Smoked
  Salmon, 124
TRUE COD (see COD)
TUNA
Curried tuna, 43
Simple tuna salad, 60
Salad Nicoise, 61
TURBOT
General information, 29
How to buy, 29
How to cook, 29

Other Books By Frank Amato Publications

American Nymph Fly Tying Manual, by Randall Kaufmann, $9.95

An Angler's Astoria, by Dave Hughes, $9.95

Complete Book of Western Hatches, by R. Hafele & D. Hughes, $18.95

Columbia River Gorge, by Marty Sherman, $7.95 sb, $18.95 hb

Curtis Creek Manifesto, by Sheridan Anderson, $5.00

Do It Yourself Rod Building, by Bill Stinson, $6.95

Fishing the High Country, by Trey Combs, $3.00

Fly Patterns of Alaska, by The Alaska Flyfishers Club, $11.95

Fly Rod Steelhead, by Bill Stinson, $8.95

Greased Line Fishing for Salmon [and Steelhead], by Jock Scott, $9.95

John Day River Guide, by Art Campbell, $9.95

Kamloops, by Steve Raymond, $9.95

Lake Fishing With a Fly, by R. Kaufmann & R. Cordes, $19.95

Meanest Fish On Earth, by Larry Leonard, $5.95

Native Trout of North America, by R. H. Smith, $15.00 sb, $28.00 hb

Sea-Run, by Les Johnson, $9.95 sb, $14.95 hb

Sierra Trout Guide, by Ralph Cutter, $7.95

Steelhead Drift Fishing, by Bill Luch, $5.95

Steelhead Fly Fishing and Flies, by Trey Combs, $13.95

Steelhead Fly Tying Manual, by Tom Light & Neal Humphrey, $9.95

Tying and Fishing the West's Best dry Flies, by Wilson & Parks, $9.95

FRANK AMATO PUBLICATIONS
Box 02112, Portland, Oregon 97202
Order by phone or mail — MasterCard, Visa
(503) 653-8108